MEMORIES

Marita Littauer

HARVEST HOUSE PUBLISHERS
Eugene, Oregon 97402

HOMEMADE MEMORIES

Copyright © 1991 by Marita Littauer
Published by Harvest House Publishers
Eugene, Oregon 97402

Library of Congress Cataloging-in-Publication Data

Littauer, Marita.
    Homemade memories / Marita Littauer.
    ISBN 0-89081-862-2
    1. Entertaining.   2. Cookery.   I. Title.
TX731.L574   1991
642'.4—dc20   90-23657
                                                                CIP

Printed in the United States of America.

To my mother, Florence Littauer, for teaching me the basics of cooking and hospitality.

To my father, Fred Littauer, for teaching me how to do it all right.

To my husband, Chuck Noon, for bearing with me while we develop our own memories and for tasting and approving all the recipes featured in HomeMade Memories.

CONTENTS

Foreword by Florence Littauer

Introduction

CONTENTS

PART FIVE: MENU

FOREWORD

From the time Marita was a little girl she has had a fascination with the kitchen and a love of parties. I would gather season centerpieces and decorations and Marita loved to pull out the Easter eggs, the May baskets, the pumpkin place mats, or the Christmas napkin rings. She had a flair for decorating and she enjoyed putting her personal touch on the table settings.

There were times when she was helping me prepare a meal that I knew I could have done it much faster without her help, but I kept teaching her how to cook. Her favorite cookbooks were those that had colored pictures of the finished products. She wanted to make hers look just like the picture.

By her teen years Marita was able to prepare and present a gourmet meal, and make it all come out at the right time—a skill that many women never learn.

Little did I know as we made Christmas cookies together in her childhood that someday Marita would be teaching cooking classes on television, or writing a book on homemade memories. The hospitality and menus Marita shares in *HomeMade Memories* come right out of her own life and experience. To my delight, I have been a sampler of many of her creations.

I hope you will be inspired and motivated as you have fun with this book. If you have children, I hope you will take the time to teach them genuine hospitality as well. Nothing is quite so rewarding as creating memories with those you love.

—Florence Littauer

INTRODUCTION

—————— ❧ ——————

Gone are the days of needing to impress others and be seen in the right places. The stuffy restaurants serving fancy plates with a swirl of sauce and a morsel of meat have been replaced by a quiet dinner at home with a hearty helping of real food. The July 23, 1990 issue of *Time* magazine declares that "after the glitzy '80's cheaper and careful are back in style." It says that novelle cuisine is out and old-fashioned meat and potatoes are in. In the November 1990 issue of the English magazine *Home & Gardens*, food writer Steven Wheeler says, "The traditional homemade cake is proving an unbeatable stayer in the rat race of modern fare." I have found anything "homemade" to be a real "stayer." That's why we need homemade memories. We no longer need to impress: We aim to enjoy.

That is the entire theme behind *HomeMade Memories*, not to impress but to enjoy. Enjoy your home. Enjoy your food. Enjoy your family and friends.

HomeMade Memories centers around the table: the kitchen table, the dining room table, and the picnic table. The table is the spot where real life takes place. Sitting around the table enjoying a good meal provides an atmosphere of relaxation and a comfortable environment. Conversations happen around the table that we would never take time for if it weren't for our meals. The time seems to fly by. A recent magazine ad for Wedgewood tableware says, "Good food, good wine, good company. Good gracious, is it that time?" Have you ever noticed how the words "Let's move into the living room" change the tone of conversation and usually end the evening? People who were excitedly discussing the next election go mute with the move. Children who were having fun over the fudge cake look sleepy when they are lined up on the living room sofa. So let's stay where we can laugh together, review our schedules, and listen to each other's stories.

Yes, let's sit around the table where we can listen, laugh, live, and love, for this is where memories are made.

HomeMade Memories is for real people. People who don't have time to spend in the kitchen like grandma did, but who long for the warmth and laughter that her kitchen provided. It is for people who wish they had more time with their kids and for friends who wish they could spend some quality time together and just talk without the formality of an official meeting. It is for busy people who don't see enough of their friends and miss the special bond that social fellowship provides.

HomeMade Memories is for the person who has great memories of childhood, the person who remembers those special times around the table and is ready to recapture those qualities in his or her own home. It is also for the person who doesn't have those special memories, whose childhood was torn and traumatic, where Norman Rockwell pictures appeared only on "Father Knows Best" and "The Brady Bunch." Regardless of your background, positive or not, you can begin now to create homemade memories for the future.

Homemade memories can be made anywhere that people call "home": in the apartment of a single man or woman, in the condominium that roommates share, in the bungalow of the couple who are building traditions together. And of course, homemade memories are for families, big and small, families with little kids, big kids, and grandkids. Homemade memories are for you!

Memories

&

———— ❦ ————

Chapter 1

A Lifetime of Memories

———— ❦ ————

Sometimes life at home seems too filled with the mandatory and the mundane. We must brush our teeth and we must take a bath. Laundry needs to be done and the floors need to be swept. But home is more than just a place to change clothes and get some sleep. Home is a place for memories to be made. These homemade memories are there for us to reach for and rely upon when life is at risk of losing its meaning.

Oliver Wendell Holmes said, "Where we love is home, home that our feet may leave, but not our hearts." My feet often leave home. I am frequently flying off to one place or another to teach a seminar or speak at a banquet, and while people often envy the places I visit, the place I love is always home. Anyone who travels frequently will tell you that the best part of traveling is coming home. My feet may leave, but never my heart.

What makes home such a special place is that real life is lived there. It is not fiction and it doesn't need to be fancy. It's real and relaxing, a refuge and a retreat. Robert Frost wrote, "Home is where, when you go, they have to take you in." It should be the place we would most like to be. Where we know we'll be taken in and received with love.

I remember how pleased I was when Chuck came home early one day. He told me all the guys at the office were going out after work and he should have gone with them to be sociable but when it came time to get in the car, the only place he really wanted to go was "home." It isn't the size of the house that makes it home. It may be an apartment or a condo but it can still be "home." Yes, home is where you feel welcome, where they have to take you in.

Memories Can Be Made Anywhere

Our current home consists of a house that we and the bank own. It is not a big house, just 1450 square feet consisting of two-bedrooms, no family room, and a den which Chuck uses as an office. It is a nice little house in a starter neighborhood. Almost all of us are in our first houses and each Saturday morning the air is filled with a buzz as we all mow our first yards. We know when anyone adds a new tree or builds a patio cover.

My family is made up of myself, my husband, Chuck, our fluffy schnauzer dogs, Nikita and Nantucket, and my nephew's rabbit, Curious George, who has lived with us since we got married. In the past our home has been a rented condo in La Costa with a view of the famous golf course and the lagoon, another condo in North Hollywood where our only view was a stoplight at the major intersection where we lived, an apartment in Redlands with fake brick kitchen flooring and awful high-low brown carpet that was only low in spots, and a tiny 850-square-foot condo that I owned when we got married. Our memories have been made in homes we loved and places I hated but I have good memories from every one!

Memories Are Made with Family

In addition I have homemade memories from my childhood. Our family's first home was a large ranch house in North Haven, Connecticut, with a backyard of rolling hills. I lived there with my parents, my older sister, my little brother, and assorted pets.

When we moved to California I was nine years old. Our home went from being a large ranch house to a little three-bedroom bungalow on the grounds of Campus Crusade for Christ. There were lots of us then. The regular family of five was joined by many others. Gudren was from Germany and came as a "mother's helper." My cousin's family was going through a difficult time so Dwayne lived with us for a year. In addition, Dolores, my father's secretary, shared our home for a year. Many visiting speakers, authors, and missionaries also crowded in around our dinner table. People like Hal Lindsey as his ministry was just starting and Josh McDowell, when he was young and single, were a regular part of our lives. We have some wonderful memories from that little bungalow.

Memories Are Made with Friends

From there all of us except Dolores and Dwayne moved to a big custom home in the foothills of San Bernardino. This one had six bedrooms and fewer people! My parents had built this home to be a center for ministry. It had a large family room that would seat 100 people and often did. It had a wall of glass that looked out over the pool and on to the San Bernardino National Forest. Many of my Pioneer Girl and youth group events took place in that pool on the hill.

Every inch of that big house was well used as the extra beds were often full and there were large Bible studies or dinners going on as often as several times a week. My father, being the organized melancholy that he is, arranged all the details. If your last name started with A through K you would bring a salad one week. If your name began with L through R, you would bring a main dish, and if you were at the end of the alphabet you would bring dessert. The next week the cycle would rotate—the early part of the alphabet would bring a main course and so on. Everyone had to bring the recipe to display with their item. My mother, being a flamboyant sanguine and needing all the pretty things, made matching tablecloths and napkins out of sheets for every table we could round up. Since my father had been in the restaurant business we had enough silverware and plates for the hundred or so guests we had each week. We all worked to set the whole house up so that it looked nice. My father greeted the people and told them where to go with their food. After dinner everyone moved into the large family room for the

Bible study time. I got much of my Christian training sitting under the teaching of my parents and the other Christian leaders who came through our home.

Memories Are Made Outside

After ten years in the big house we moved to a little condo right off the main boulevard in Redlands. All night long my parents listened to the cars as they thump, thump, thumped over the concrete sections of pavement. Our family now consisted of Mom, Dad, Fred, me, and Brenda. Brenda, a Campus Crusade staffer, and I shared one room, Fred had a room, and my parents had a room. There was no family room and only one eating area. After the big house it seemed like we were all over each other. Although this little condo is the smallest place my family ever lived it is where my fondest memories come from. We had to get a little more creative there and the size demanded that we spend more time together. There was a small patio in the front with a lattice-type patio cover and a little rock waterfall. Large ferns and other lush plants grew there. My favorite memories revolve around that patio. We ate almost all of our meals there, and I can remember all of us sitting out there morning after morning talking and laughing away. At dinner we were often there until long after sunset when the chilly air chased us inside and back to the reality of the dishes.

Memories Are Made at the Table

After a few years we all moved down the street to a bigger house. It was long and low and big enough for entertaining but by now I was finishing up college and starting my own business as a color consultant. My mother had written her first several books and had a fairly full speaking schedule. She had an office in town and people who had read her books would frequently stop by her office for help or advice. Since her third book was on marriage, many of the people that came to see her had marriage problems and she would sometimes share situations with us as dinner table conversation. We never knew who the people were, but we all made our contributions to solving their problems. It became like a contest to see who could come up with the best advice and our combined answer was often the suggestion that my mother gave them the next time they called. Today the dinnertime conversation of my youth has become a great help to me. Since we discussed all the normal marriage difficulties I am better prepared to face the rough spots that come up in my own marriage. I'll catch myself about to say something that I'd later regret when one of those conversations about marriage pops into my mind. I bite my tongue, think it through, and solve the problem before it becomes a big issue. Discussing marriages must have prepared us for marriage rather than discouraged us because both Brenda and I got married out of that house.

The table has always been a central part of my family and when I look back on my childhood memories its importance in my life is very clear. I am sure that my current interest in making the mealtime special has come from the fellowship and fun we enjoyed as children.

My memory banks are filled with homemade memories. When I am feeling sad or lonely I just have to reach into my basket of memories and I can pull out an entire bouquet of great times. I set them on the table and they brighten my life like a fresh bunch of daisies.

You have the opportunity to create memories for yourself and your family. It is never too late to get started. You can begin now to add memories to your bouquet. It doesn't matter if your home is big or small. You don't have to be a great cook or a perfect hostess. Just relax and have a good time.

Chapter 2

—— ❧ ——

Making Memories Today

—— ❧ ——

*I*t has been said, "By means of an image we are often able to hold on to our lost belongings. But it is the desperateness of losing them which picks the flowers of memory and binds the bouquet." Each of us have positive images of days and events from our past. The events themselves are long since gone, but the images stay on in our minds and become the flowers of our memory. While there are bound to be some negative memories in our bouquet, like thorns on a rose, they are not why we pick out the memory. The memories that we reach for over and over again are the good times and the special events in our lives. The goal of *HomeMade Memories* is to help you fill your bouquet with pretty flowers and great times that you'll never want to lose. The best memories are those that are picked from your own garden, the memories that are homemade.

Childhood Memories

The memories of your childhood may be full of good times like mine. You may remember special family gatherings with all the aunts and uncles present. Your memory may be filled with warm kitchen scenes and spirited conversation around the table. I clearly remember the Thanksgiving back in Connecticut when, instead of preparing the traditional Thanksgiving turkey, my mother made individual Cornish game hens for all of us. I was thrilled and thought it was great that we each got our own "turkey." To this day I have a warm spot in my heart for Cornish game hens and I've included a favorite recipe for them in the "After Work Company Dinner" menu.

Making Time for Togetherness

In my family the table was always a sacred place, a place for conversation and encouragement. As we got older and life got busier we were not able to have dinner together as often, but the table remained sacred. Our special meal became breakfast instead of dinner. Every morning my father got up before the rest of us and prepared a real breakfast. Not just dry cereal or juice and toast. He cooked a real breakfast every day. Sometimes it was eggs, bacon, and English muffins. Other times it was pancakes or French toast. Sometimes we had hot cereal, but that wasn't very popular. The best breakfast of all was "skinnies." We baby boomers would call them crepes but in my family they'll always be "skinnies," short for skinny pancakes. We had them on special occasions and weekends. They would usually be served just like a rolled-up pancake with butter and warm, real maple syrup. Sometimes there would be yogurt, fresh fruit, or whipped cream to go with them. I'm not really a breakfast person, but it is hard to stay in bed with the smell of bacon or pancakes wafting through the air. Dad would ring the chimes and play some silly tune. When we heard the notes we knew that breakfast would be on the table in one minute! We scrambled out of bed and arrived at the table in a variety of disheveled states. It was there at the breakfast table that we would laugh, joke, plan our days, and get fed both physically and emotionally. We would start with the blessing and take turns asking God to bless the food. It was not a time for teaching or correction, but a time for encouragement and warmth.

As I speak on this subject people frequently tell me they don't eat together anymore because they all have different schedules. If eating together is important to you, try squeezing in a good breakfast. It's so much easier to bounce out of bed when you hear the hum of the orange juicer in your ear and smell the aroma of bacon wafting through the air!

Breakfast is also a special time for Chuck and me, but because of our work schedules we have it only on weekends. If my parents are in town we happily troop over to their house for the favored "Father Fred Breakfast." Chuck has not taken on the same affection for cooking breakfast that my father has, so I am usually the breakfast cook when my parents are away. While I don't have Dad's innate breakfast knack, my buttermilk pancakes, homemade biscuits, and whole-grain waffles are very popular.

Our special daily meal together is dinner. I always set the table nicely with a tablecloth or placemats and as my mother and Emilie Barnes have taught me, I always use cloth napkins. If my roses are in bloom I have a bouquet on the table, and I specially select the dishes and silverware to be compatible with the meal. I do this not because I am a snob who needs to have it that way but because I want our time together to be memorable. In fact while I write this I am eating dinner by myself while Chuck is in school. I am having potato chips and onion dip. The bag of chips is on the table, and the dip is in a plastic container. It's okay for me but I would never serve Chuck like that. If Chuck had to choose between going out with the guys each night or coming home to me, I would want him to choose me! A good, fresh, hot meal, served with love and homemade apple pie is hard to turn down. It is similar to my childhood experience. When I was a kid I never craved breakfast, but I made the effort to get there because it was a very special daily event.

Good Times Offer Balance

I believe that when life at home is good, all the other things in life can be terrible and we can still smile and carry on. But when life at home is unpleasant and out of order, the slightest upset in the rest of our lives can be devastating. When everything is great between Chuck and me, I can have a bad day at work, get a speeding ticket, and break a nail and when I come home everything will still be fine. But if I head off to work mad, I can be sure that the computer will eat my entire mailing list and I'll burst into tears. Life at home is worth taking the time to make special. You deserve the strength you'll draw from your efforts, your spouse wants it, and your children need it. It has been proven over and over again that children who come from a strong, healthy home environment do better in school and in all of life.

Make Good Times from the Bad

If you know my mother's story, you know she and her two brothers grew up in the Great Depression. She was deprived of a normal house and grew up in three rooms behind her father's store. All five of her family slept in one room and bathed in the kitchen sink. They didn't have a nice house, good dishes, or even cloth napkins. What they did have was a loving home that centered around the table. Their table was in the center of the store where they all ate together, taking turns to get up and wait on a customer. For a fancy company meal they put the milk bottle under the table instead of on it. In that unlikely setting for excellence my mother and my two uncles were challenged with creativity and conversation. Today all three of those children have reached the top of their chosen professions, and they all make their living talking—as a speaker and writer, a minister, and a morning drive-time radio personality.

Even if you didn't grow up in a home with a nurturing atmosphere you don't need to miss out on it today. You can begin now to make your home the place your family wants it to be. You can create homemade memories for yourself, your family, and your friends. Start to do the things that make a meal special. Cook fresh foods, set a pretty table, and have enjoyable, encouraging conversation. When you do that you will be filling the bouquet of your memory with bright flowers that don't wilt or fade with time.

Chapter 3

❧

Preserving the Bouquet

❧

No matter how wonderful the memories might be, like flowers in a vase, they all tend to wilt with time. To keep memories fresh it is important to develop some way to enhance our own natural capacity to remember. I have three techniques I use as floral preservative for my memories. In the process of making memories for yourself and your family you may be able to adapt these same systems.

When Chuck and I got married we received two gifts that have become treasure chests of memories to me.

The first gift was a guest book given to us by my mother. You may have formal stuffy thoughts about guest books. I picture most of them as having gold edges inside thick leather or leatherlike binding. The book my mother gave me was navy blue with a calico print on the outside. The front cover shows an inviting scene with a fireplace and a wing chair. It's called "The Joy of Remembering Our Guests." Right off it seemed more inviting than the intimidating versions I remembered.

When I was in my early teens we used to visit a family that lived near us. The minute we were in the door the guest book was thrust into our hands and we were asked to sign in. It felt somewhat like going to the doctor's office; we had to sign in before we could have a visit.

Despite that experience I began to use my guest book when I had company. Not for every person who walked through the door as our friends had done, but whenever I had really worked to create a special meal or there was a special event; whenever there was something memorable. When the gathering was about to end I would bring out the guest book. At first I felt silly asking my guests to sign my guest book and I brought it out hesitantly. But after I'd begun to use it, I learned to appreciate its usefulness in memory enhancement. Now I bring it out with no apology.

By asking my guests to sign my book after the gathering was over I found they seldom wrote just their names and addresses as most books ask for. Instead they made comments about the evening. Today I still keep that same guest book on a table by my front door. When I am waiting for someone to come by for something or if I am just feeling down or lonely, I like to sit in my wing chair by the fireplace and flip through its pages. When I look at the names, the dates, and the comments that are included there, the memory of the event comes right back to me.

The very first entry in my guest book is a surprise birthday party I threw for Chuck when we'd been married for only three months. I wanted so much to be a good wife and I was sure this was the thing to do. Chuck had a little Rolodex on his dresser. I went through it and invited everyone that was a male or a couple. (I didn't invite any women, lest they be old girlfriends. Since we'd only dated five months and been engaged just two weeks I thought there might still be some of them in the Rolodex!) I made cute invitations and had everyone RSVP to my office. It was going to be a great party and Chuck had no idea! Being the kind of person who likes everyone and assumes everyone loves me, it never occurred to me that Chuck might not want everyone in his Rolodex to be in our home. Worse yet, I didn't tell these people Chuck preferred they not bring gifts. To me a birthday party is not a birthday party without presents!

All those people are recorded as the first entries in my guest book. As I look at it now the entire memory comes back as if it were yesterday. While Chuck was furious with me at the time, we both now laugh over my eagerness and his stubbornness and it has become a good memory.

Brenda, who used to live with my family, and her husband, Ken, were at that party. In addition to their name they wrote, "Your place looks great, so does Chuck!" My favorite grandmother, who has since passed away, wrote her name and then after it in parenthesis wrote "Grammie." She lived only a couple of months after that and I'm so glad my guest book has recorded that entry, "Grammie."

Needless to say I have never had another surprise party for Chuck, and I let him know that if he ever gave a party for me and told people not to bring presents he'd be in big trouble!

I smile every time I read the names in the guest book for October 30, 1983. It was the surprise party Chuck threw for me a few months after his. It was a Sunday and I had to go to work for the afternoon. I was doing color analysis then and a lady was coming to my office to have her colors done. Chuck had never really seen what I do and I decided it would be a good time for him to take me to work and stay with me for the hour-and-a-half consultation. I asked him what he had planned for the afternoon and he gave me a weak list of activities he might do while I was gone. It was obvious that none of those things were very important, and I began to insist he come with me. He refused and I got mad, but my client was due any minute so I stuck on a happy face and stormed off to the office. Two hours later I returned and was greeted by all my friends holding gifts and shouting "surprise," and suddenly I understood. Chuck had pulled the whole thing off and I never had a clue.

Get yourself a guest book and begin collecting lifetime memories. Try to find a nice friendly one like mine rather than a formal, intimidating one with gold edges. Keep it right by the front door where you will see it as guests come and go so you won't forget to have them sign it. To start off you might want to have a couple of friends sign it and add comments like "That was the best meal I've ever had" or "You are the hostess with the mostess" so that others will get the idea. It is those extra comments that really make the book fun to read. I frequently see my guests going through the previous pages and chuckling to themselves as they read the fun things others have written.

Christmas Memories

On the second page of my guest book are the names of Bob and Emilie Barnes. They came to our first home for Christmas dinner. Emilie wrote, "Your home is warm and loving. Thank You! Hugs." They brought with them my second gift of memory enhancement. It is a book that Emilie now sells at all her seminars, and I recommend it as a perfect wedding gift. It is a simple red book with green lettering and a green wreath on the cover. It is called the *Family Christmas Book*. It has a two-page spread for each year with a place to write down the year and the location where you celebrated Christmas, a spot for a photo of the occasion, and room for listing those people who joined the celebration. I used to just write in the names myself but now I have everyone sign in, like the guest book. It has been fun to see my nieces' and nephews' handwriting change as they mature. There is a place to write in special memories of Christmas and of the past year. At the end there is a spot to include your Christmas card. Since my Christmas card always includes a letter that recaps the past year I use the entire space provided for writing to help me remember that Christmas. Our Christmases always have something special to remember.

On Christmas Day, 1986, I prepared a sit-down dinner for 15 people in our little two-bedroom rented condo in La Costa. We were jammed in everywhere. It had started out small: Chuck and me, his mother, and my parents. I invited my sister and her family and my brother and a date, but I never really thought they would come since they live an hour and a half away from us. Then I invited Aunt Jean to come west for the Christmas season and she accepted. A friend of my mother's called and she and her son had no place to go for Christmas so my mother invited them to join us. Everyone came! We put the leaves in the table and borrowed chairs. We were seated so tightly there was no chance of getting up without disrupting everyone. My sister brought a card table and chairs, and one group used them to sit in front of the fireplace. My great aunt ended up sitting outdoors on the patio with my two older nephews. I was very glad Christmas in California is warm enough to still enjoy outdoor dining!

Because I didn't have enough room in the kitchen to prepare all the food, I planned the menu and sent everyone a recipe as their mealtime assignment. I made the Cornish game hens; a whole hen for everyone. I had to buy those throwaway aluminum pans because I didn't have enough roasting pans. My mother-in-law brought the rolls and my sister was assigned the vegetables. Aunt Jean made the salad and my mother and father brought beverages. My brother and his date stopped at Bakers Square and picked up a few pies. It all worked and we had a great time.

I had noticed a moving truck out front and felt sorry for whoever it was that had to be moving on Christmas day. I went out and invited them to join us. In a little while our new neighbors Chip and Cindy joined the group for some refreshment.

I didn't need a big house to make that Christmas special. It wasn't the lavish meal; it was the friends and family that made the memories. We don't live in that little condo anymore, but its memories still live on in my Christmas book. I have a picture of every-one jammed around the table and the whole story written out so I won't forget.

Aunt Jean was with us for two weeks and somehow she escaped back to Massachusetts without signing the guest book. I sent it to her with a preaddressed envelope and enough postage for her to return it without having to go to the post office. She wrote, "12/18/86–1/7/87, Aunt Jean. A delightful 'no prob-lem' vacation. I loved the TLC, the great food, the chance to see all the family!"

A guest book and the *Christmas Family Book* are great ways to preserve your memories. You can buy them or make your own, but if you want to keep your homemade memories these books are a great way to do it. The Christmas book has enough space for 25 years of memories. What a treasure it will be when the 25 years are up!

A Photographic Memory

The third thing I do to help preserve my memories is to take plenty of pictures. I often joke that I should have stock in Kodak! There are a lot of people who take pictures—they take scenic pictures of trees and flowers or surprise shots of an entire group caught off-guard. While those pictures may be fun or pretty, they do little to enhance your memories of special events. At first you'll need to give a little thought to your picture taking. Don't think of it as art, but rather as documenting the occasion. Think of the things you are going to want to remember later on and then take pictures of those things, places, and people. If I am having a special dinner gathering and

I put extra effort into setting the table, I'll take a picture of the table before everyone arrives. While we are all eating and having a great time, I have everyone stop for a moment and smile for the camera. I document the occasion.

My last Christmas was well documented. We had a full house again. The Smarts were with us. I had met John and his wife while we were teaching a seminar for his company in Australia. They told me they were bringing the family to America for a "holiday" in December. I invited them to stay with us and join our family for Christmas. I couldn't let them eat Christmas dinner at Denny's.

Six of them came the week before Christmas and, although our little house was crowded, we had a great time together. The girls loved the bunny and the dogs ran Michael ragged. I have adorable pictures of Katherine and Rosemary snuggled in the hide-a-bed with Curious George, my rabbit. Alison was an especially sweet, sensitive little girl. She and Nikita really hit it off, and I have the most precious picture of them sitting in the backyard.

We sent the Smarts off each day with maps, tour books, and discount coupons to see the sights. They returned each night excited but exhausted. One of their most important endeavors while in America was to be sure each of the children got a pair of Reeboks, a luxury item in Australia. The day they arrived home heavily laden with packages from the Foot Locker was a major event and one worthy of documentation.

On the actual day of Christmas we all ended up at my parents' house for a great time of gift-giving and Christmas turkey with all the trimmings. We have numerous pictures to enhance our memory of that special occasion.

If you're new to photography you'll soon find that most people do better if they use a simple, one-button type of camera to take pictures of memorable family events. My friend Connie has very few pictures of the special events in her home because her only camera is too difficult for her to use. If everyone has to hold still while the camera is focused and the light meter read, they will quickly tire of picture taking and groan at any future documentation attempts. Even my husband, Chuck, who has his undergraduate degree in photography, takes almost all of his pictures with my Canon Sure Shot. Get a camera you can use easily. If you don't have a natural flair for photography be sure the camera has an auto focus feature and auto flash. A timer is a nice additional feature that allows you to be in the picture too.

Above our fireplace we have a beautiful 20 x 36-inch picture with Chuck and me in the foreground and the village of Grafton, Vermont, nestled in the valley below. The leaves on the trees are rich in their October colors and the white church spires of this tiny village reach toward the sky. Everyone who visits our home comments on that photograph. They ask, "Who took that picture?" They are so surprised when we answer, "The camera." We put the camera on a post, I posed, Chuck pushed the button and then ran to get into the picture. We felt silly standing there in the hills smiling to ourselves but because of the timer we have a beautiful memory of our trip.

Once you have a number of pictures, it will be easier for you and your family to relive your memories if you put them into an album of some type. You might want to take an evening and sort through the last few months' pictures. First sort them by event, and through the combined use of your guest book and personal calendar figure out when each event took place. Put each grouping in a rubber band and stack them chronologically. Then use a paint pen to label the front of the pictures with names, dates, and any cute or clever comments that will add to the picture. The paint pens work especially well because they are opaque and can be easily read even when they are used over a busy photo. Metallic colors such as silver work well on both light-colored and dark-colored pictures. The paint pens can be found at most art or office supply stores. Be sure you get the fine-tip type of paint pen so you can label the pictures without covering up the entire photo.

By writing directly on the photo you save space in your album and you don't have to worry about the label falling out of the album and getting lost. When you label only the back of the picture as many people do, a person flipping through the album has no clue of who or what is in the picture. There is nothing worse than being held captive while someone plods through their photo album and explains in detail the story behind each shot. When the pictures are labeled other people can enjoy and understand them without a complete tour through the album. If you ever need a "pure" picture that is not labeled you still have the negatives and can easily have an additional picture made.

Start with the pictures one event at a time and label them. If you are using paint pens, be sure to lay the pictures out and allow them to dry for about ten minutes before you stack them on top of each other and before you put them into the album. I have learned the hard way that stacking them too soon will smear the paint and ruin the pictures.

Once all the pictures are labeled, put them in the album starting with the earliest event and filling the album in chronological order. This way you'll be able to go back years later and relive those memories and events of the past. While the memories might fade, the photos will always be there as a reminder. Keep the photo albums out where you, your family, and your friends can easily enjoy them.

I have lots of memories that have been made at home. Whenever I am feeling lonely, sorry for myself, or just plain depressed I reach into my mind and pull out a bouquet of memories to brighten my day. With the combination of a guest book, *Family Christmas Book*, and photo album, you too can have a bouquet of memories that will never fade.

Mood

Chapter 4

❦

The Frame for Your Art

❦

When I was 13 years old my mother began speaking at Christian Women's Clubs, mother/daughter banquets, and women's retreats. I was frequently able to join her as we traveled to different cities and states. We often had a meal or even spent the night in other people's homes and I received a broad education in the different ways people live. There was one occasion that sticks in my mind and influences my mealtimes even today.

My mother had been speaking during the day at the church where Mrs. Lintz was the Director of Women's Ministries. She had invited us over to her home for dinner after the event was over. While my mother was in the living room with some of the other ladies from the committee, I went into the kitchen and offered to help Mrs. Lintz. She asked me to help her set the table and together we went to the cupboard where she kept the tablecloths. As she was looking for just the right tablecloth, she told me that this particular tablecloth had been a wedding gift. She had never used it when her children were young because it was "too good" and she was afraid they might ruin it. Now that they were all grown and out of the house she had been waiting for a special occasion to use it. Our presence in her home was that occasion.

She proudly took the tablecloth out of the cupboard. But when she opened it up and placed it on the table, Mrs. Lintz gasped. This tablecloth that was *too* good for her own family was now *no* good! The tablecloth had been folded up in that cupboard for over 20 years. One edge had been exposed all these years, and as we unfolded it that exposed edge disintegrated and crumbled to dust on the table.

It truly had been a lovely tablecloth and she was right to save it for a special occasion. But it is sad to think that in over 20 years of marriage Mrs. Lintz hadn't ever used that tablecloth. Now it could never be used for the lovely meal it was meant to present.

Nothing Is Too Good

I learned a valuable lesson from Mrs. Lintz's tragedy that day. I learned nothing should be "too good" for my family. If I use a lovely tablecloth only once and it gets ruined, at least we have had the opportunity to enjoy it once. When I use my good crystal and I break a glass, I shrug and say to myself, "At least I got to enjoy it for a little while."

I hope that, like me, you will learn from Mrs. Lintz. Don't wait for a worthy guest to use the special things you have in your home. Save the special things for special occasions. That is part of what *makes* an occasion special. Yet no one is more special than your family and it is important they be treated that way. I am not suggesting you be foolish and give a two-year-old a crystal goblet of your grandmother's, but I do recommend you use your grandmother's crystal goblets from time to time. Get the good things out and enjoy them.

As I have been the "company" in many homes I have heard children exclaim, "Mommy why don't we use these pretty dishes more often?" The older children will lean over and say, "Mom only gets out the good dishes when company comes." In many homes the standard table setting is a plastic tablecloth or plastic placemats, plastic plates, paper napkins, and flatware that has just been plopped at each place or even just tossed onto the middle of the table. This casual and unelaborate type of table setting is fine for a meal like a peanut butter sandwich and some potato chips, but it hardly sets the mood for a memorable event.

In making homemade memories I suggest you treat your family like company. I was on a radio program recently talking about hospitality. The host kept wanting me to talk about entertaining "company" and I kept bringing up my theory: You don't reserve "hospitality" or "entertaining" for "company." No one should be more important than your family. If you treat your family like "company," then when guests visit they become just like the family. There shouldn't be a real difference between a "company meal" and a "family dinner."

Setting a Special Table

Don't use your good tableware just for company. Let your family know how important they are. Decide when to get out the special dishes, glasses, tablecloths, and napkins based on the type of meal being served rather than on the people being served. If you have just slapped together a few sandwiches and opened a bag of chips, the good china hardly seems appropriate. Use paper or plastic plates and paper napkins. But if you are serving a real meal, allow the table settings to be the frame for your artwork. The table settings "set" the mood.

For a meal such as pot roast, stew, chowder, or baked beans that is hearty and homespun use stoneware-type dishes even if it is a "company meal." Set the table with heavy or rustic placemats and matching napkins. Use your everyday silverware and regular tumblers. A centerpiece for these homey meals might be a small houseplant or potted flowers. When your family and/or guests smell the warm fragrance of the food and see the attractive table they will know they are in for a special time.

If the meal is more elegant get out the "good" dishes, even if it is just for the family. One of my favorite meals is the Sherried Chicken Dinner. It takes about 45 minutes to prepare and it tastes like a real gourmet treat. The boneless chicken breasts are sautéed with butter, glazed with a sherry sauce, and served with wild rice and steamed asparagus with lemon butter. For dessert I suggest Chocolate Mousse. Even though this meal is quick to prepare, it is very elegant. I often cook this entire dinner when I'm serving only Chuck and myself. When I set the table I use the lovely lace placemats that Chuck's Aunt Margaret gave us. They are white lace with a light blue fabric underneath and they have matching light blue napkins. I put the napkins in silver napkin rings and I use my "good" silverware, the "good" china, and my crystal goblets. For the centerpiece I light tall candles in crystal candle holders and put a single rose in a bud vase. This doesn't have to be a "company" dinner; the table settings can add to the mood and turn a quick dinner into a romantic evening.

A few years ago I found some glass dishes I liked in a mail-order catalog. My parents had some plain glass dishes and I have always liked the clean feeling of the clear glass. The dishes I found were reproductions of antique cut-glass plates, bowls, and glasses. They were very reasonably priced at about $20 for 12 plates, bowls, or glasses so I got a basic set. For the last several years my sister has been adding to my collection for my birthday and each Christmas. You might want to do as I did and add tabletop items to your gift list. I think I now have the full set including matching salt and pepper shakers, cream and sugar, and a butter dish.

These clear glass dishes are perfect for a light meal. I usually use them to serve breakfast or a delicate meal such as quiche and fruit salad. In keeping with the light theme, in addition to my clear glass plates I use the "good" silverware, pretty floral placemats and napkins, and my favorite bunny napkin rings. Depending on the meal I use either the tumblers or the goblets which are a part of that collection. For breakfast I serve the orange juice in the goblets and with quiche I serve the milk or water in the tumblers. Either fresh-cut flowers or silk flowers would be a perfect centerpiece for a light, fresh meal.

While it is doubtful that you have the exact same collection of dishes I have, you can still use my ideas. Look over the dishes, glasses, silverware, place-mats, napkins, and tablecloths you have. If you only have one set of dishes and silverware, you can still vary the mood through a creative use of tablecloths or placemats, napkins, napkin rings, and center-pieces. These extras don't have to be costly or lavish. In fact low-cost options, such as using a twin sheet for the tablecloth and making matching napkins out of a set of pillow cases, are often the most durable and easiest to care for. Sheets that are a cotton-polyester blend will wash and dry beautifully with-out needing to be ironed.

The napkins can be made out of sheets or pur-chased ready-made, but they should be cloth. They are so much nicer to use and are more economical and ecological. You buy them once and use them over and over again. The cloth napkins can usually be used for several meals before needing to be washed. Just leave them in the napkin ring at each person's place. When the person sits down in his spot for the next meal, his napkin is there. When the napkins get dirty simply exchange them for clean ones and wash the others with your regular laundry.

As long as you are going to make the extra effort of setting the table nicely, why not do something special with the napkins? You could just fold them and place the napkin under the fork and sometimes I do just that. But you could make the table so much prettier by using napkin rings for a festive touch. They can be as simple as a piece of wide ribbon tied around the napkin or as ornate as sterling silver or cut crystal. I collect bunnies and I have been given several different types of bunny napkin rings. I have white ceramic bunnies that sit crouched and regal-looking for more formal meals, cute cartoon-like bunnies that I use on the patio, and pewter bunnies that provide for an elegant look. I have also seen attractive napkin rings made out of a wide piece of PVC plastic plumbing pipe, the kind you use for your sprinklers. The pipe is cut into widths of about one and one-half inches and spray-painted or covered with ribbon.

For a casual meal I simply unfold the napkin, hold it by the middle, shake it out and push it through the napkin ring. This makes it look nice and fluffy. Set the napkin and napkin ring to the left of the fork or across the top of the plate. (See table setting diagram on page 49.) To create a more formal look fold the napkin in half, lay it out lengthwise, and fold it like an accordion with one-inch folds. Push the folded napkin three-quarters of the way through the napkin ring and fan out the top half of the napkin, or push the napkin halfway through and fan both halves. With this style, place the napkin and napkin ring either on the plate or where the plate goes. For variety, or if you don't have napkin rings, unfold the napkin and hold it by the center to fluff it up, then fold the first couple of inches under and tuck the napkin into a glass so that the corners are sticking out. (See page 48 for illustrations.)

These ideas will give you simple ways to dress up your table and make the meal special. If you want to get really creative, the linen departments of most

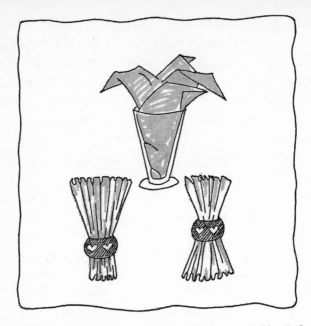

department stores have books that are full of clever napkin-folding techniques.

If there are children in your home they can easily be involved in setting the table. While I do not have children I do have nieces and nephews who visit from time to time and my little six-year-old friend, Misha, from next door is a frequent visitor. She seldom stays for dinner but she likes to be there when I am cooking. I put her to work setting the table. She picks out the placemats, napkins, and napkin rings. She loves to fluff up the napkin, put it in the napkin ring, and place it on the table. She has gotten quite good at setting the whole table. I have taught her the basics of silverware placement and she usually gets it right without my having to stand over her. I make a big fuss over what a great job she does and she thinks it is terrific.

The Basics

In case you are not sure how to set a table, keep these basics in mind. The fork goes to the left of the plate and the knife and spoon go to the right. If you are serving a salad, a main course, and a dessert that needs a fork (like pie) you may need three forks. Typically the salad and dessert forks are the same size and they are shorter and smaller than the main-course fork. You use silverware from the outside in. Since the salad is usually served first, the salad fork goes to the far left and the main course fork is next. The dessert fork is placed right next to the plate (or it can be placed above the plate). The knife is placed to the right of the plate with the blade facing in toward the plate. Usually only one spoon is placed on the table and it goes to the right of the knife. If soup is being served the soup spoon will go to the right of the regular spoon since the soup is usually eaten before the main course.

The drinking glass or goblet is placed above the knife and if a cup and saucer is used, it goes to the right of the drinking glass. The salad plate goes above the fork and if a bread and butter plate is used it goes just above and to the right of the salad plate.

These table-setting guidelines are almost universally accepted. Knowing where the different pieces belong will make you and your guests more confident.

One day a friend and I went out to lunch. The restaurant where we chose to meet had changed hands and was a fancier restaurant than we had expected, but since we were there we decided to stay. We each ordered a chef salad. There were three forks on the table and my friend was embarrassed when she had to ask me which fork to use.

I'm sure you have been at a luncheon or dinner where everyone was seated at round tables. The round shape makes it less obvious which bread plate belongs to whom. When the rolls are passed people are momentarily confused as they try to figure out where to set their bread.

To avoid this type of embarrassment remember that the drinks, a glass, or a cup and saucer go above the knife and the extra small plates, such as the salad or bread plate, go above the fork. (See diagram on page 49.)

Once you have an attractive table, you have created a beautiful frame for your meal.

A Pretty Plate

My father was in the restaurant business while I was growing up. He taught me that the food should look good on the plate and that the appearance of the meal is almost as important as the meal itself. Because of his background our meals were always served to us on the plate. Rather than serving "family style" by placing a bowl of potatoes, a plate of meat, and a platter of vegetables on the table, the main course was artfully arranged on the plate. When we were kids we often stood in line in the kitchen, picked up our plate, and took it to our seats. In my home I serve the plates for Chuck and myself in the kitchen and carry them to the table. If we have guests I do the same unless there are too many plates for me to carry, and then I have Chuck or one of the other guests help me.

I recommend you serve your meals the same way (called "formal style"). There are several benefits. A couple of the benefits are practical and some are aesthetic. By serving the meal right from the cooking containers, you avoid having an extra set of serving dishes to wash, you don't clutter up the table with a bunch of dishes, and you don't have to wait while everyone serves themselves before you eat. Additionally, the food stays hotter when you eliminate an extra step in the serving. The main aesthetic benefit is that you arrange the food and present an attractive-looking plate and your pretty table is not cluttered with unmatched dishes.

Another benefit of serving formal-style meals is that you control the portion sizes. Recently I was having guests over for dinner and somehow miscounted the number of people who would be gathered together. All week I'd been thinking about having four people for dinner. I set the table for four. I bought food for four. I was happily cooking away when one of my guests asked me why there were only four places set at the table. I gasped when I realized that there were *six* of us including Chuck and me. However, it wasn't until I served the plates that it dawned on me that I'd only bought enough food for four. But since I was serving the plates in the kitchen, I was able to divide the food into smaller portions and pass out the plates with a smile!

Because I always choose the size of the portion to be served, I let my guests know they don't have to clean their plates. Although I wouldn't force my household rules on my guests or their children, when my nieces or nephews visit I encourage them to eat several bites of each item even though they may tell me they don't like it. My parents always made us try everything on the plate and today I am so glad they did. Learning to eat things that were not my favorites has enabled me to politely and cheerfully eat escargot, sushi, and other foods I consider odd.

Memories are made around the table. An attractive table and a nicely served meal can add many flowers to your bouquet of memories.

Chapter 5

——— ❦ ———

Setting the Stage

——— ❦ ———

Setting a pretty table and preparing good food are both important parts of creating a memorable mood. But it is possible to have the best dishes and the finest food and still have an awful time at the table. The mealtime should be an event that is special and something that everyone is eager to attend. Creating a memorable mood depends on two main areas: the atmosphere in the home and the conversation that takes place around the table. When I look back on my youth I see meals that were so much fun we never wanted to miss them. My friends and the friends of my brother and sister were frequent guests at our dinner table. They seemed to show up around dinnertime and hoped to be invited to stay. They usually were. Over the years we had many people who came for dinner and stayed for weeks and even months.

However, when I visited the homes of my friends I

learned that dinner was not such a special time for every family. I remember going to a friend's home for roast beef one night. After dinner was served everyone took their plates, headed into the living room, and sat down in front of the TV. As I looked around I noticed every seat in the room faced the television set. I was used to talking during dinner but my attempts at conversation were frowned upon because I was interrupting the show.

Yes, that meal was memorable, but it wasn't a good memory. At the other extreme there are also homes where the preparation for guests is so elaborate that it takes away from the enjoyment of the occasion. Mandy's mother liked to entertain and they frequently had guests in their home for meals. In their household guests were of such importance that the whole family cleaned for days to get ready—or so it seemed to Mandy. The silver was polished and the good china and crystal were always used. The food had to be fancy and formal. By the time the guests arrived Mandy was too worn out to have a good time. When she later married and her husband wanted to invite guests in, Mandy remembered all the stress of having company and tried to avoid entertaining!

Creating a Memorable Mood

To create a mood that is positive and lasting there are several simple steps that can be taken.

First, turn the TV off. It is difficult to have a good quality time together when our attention is diverted to whatever is happening on the screen. I suggest the television and the dinner table be arranged in such a way that you can't watch TV from the table. The only time the TV should be on during a meal is if there is a special program that you make a family event of watching or if you are having a "dinner theater."

Chuck and I do not watch regular television programming in our home. It is not for religious reasons and I am not suggesting that cutting television out of life totally is for everyone, but for us it is not important. We live in a valley and the hills surrounding our home prevent us from being able to get any reception from the rabbit ears on the television. In order to get even the basic channels we need to have cable and I don't care enough about TV to pay for it. While we can't get reception on the television set, we do have one and we have a VCR. A few times a year we rent a movie and have what we call "dinner theater." We have two navy blue wing chairs that we drag to the middle of the room, facing the TV. I set the TV trays with placemats and matching cloth napkins. When dinner is ready we start the movie. When we are ready for dessert we stop the movie, clear the dishes, and get dessert ready. Then we sit back down and turn the movie back on and watch it until it is over. "Dinner theater" is usually something we do by ourselves, but sometimes we are joined by friends or neighbors who have been wanting to see the same movie. Other than making TV a special event like "dinner theater," leave the television off during mealtime.

Second, put on nice music to help create a special mood. In our home the music is Chuck's job. If we have guests he invites them to choose their favorite dinner music. I didn't know the difference between a waltz and a concerto but I have learned from

Chuck's music selection that I prefer the happy sounds of a waltz and I especially like Vivaldi's *Four Seasons*. When Chuck's nieces come for dinner they tease Chuck about his "culture." He tells them they need to learn culture and he puts on classical music. I just bought several special compact disks (CD's) from the National Public Radio catalog called Wireless. They are part of the CBS "Masterworks Dinner Classics" series. One is Christmas music and the other is brunch music. They have no words and the songs have been specially selected "to enhance a meal, yet never be intrusive."

The third step in creating a special atmosphere around the table is to eliminate as many interruptions as possible. We can't predict when someone might come to the door but we can prevent interruptions from phone calls. At our home we turn on the answering machine during dinner. If you don't have an answering machine, you can unplug the phone or turn off the ringer.

Turning off the TV, putting on nice music, and limiting interruptions set the stage for good conversation and a memorable meal. In my childhood family of talkers there was never a shortage of conversation. In fact we were all such talkers that my father had to make certain rules for dinner conversation. When I was a child I thought the rules were a little unreasonable, but now when I go to a home that doesn't follow any rules for conversational courtesy I have gained a new appreciation for my father's rules.

I am sure I didn't like his rules much because I was one of the most talkative people in the family. Being a melancholy, my father quickly divided up the number of people at the table and determined how much of the conversation was allotted to each person. When I had been monologuing and my brother had barely had a chance to talk, my father would nicely let me know I had already used up my 14 percent of the conversation and now it was time to let my brother talk.

The value of this rule is that it allows each person to have an opportunity to share what is on his or her mind and what went on in his or her day. This makes the conversation balanced and interesting.

Several years ago we were doing a CLASS seminar and the entire staff had been invited out to the home of some people in the church. This family had a large home on a farm outside of town. The food was plentiful and the large table was beautifully set. But when I look back on this evening it was one of the most unusual ones I have ever had. There was a lot of talking but no conversation. Conversation involves a sharing of ideas, a combination of talking and listening and getting better acquainted with one another.

Once the general introductions had been made around the table and the food was served, the son next to me got up and stood until he had everyone's attention. He told us he had memorized several poems just for my parents. He gave some background on each poem and began to recite.

Although he gave a moving rendition, after a while the guests became uneasy. His recitation seemed to set the tone for the evening and everything from then on was one performance after another. His father told a few stories that someone had told him. We all laughed politely. At the other end of the table the matriarch of the household told a story about a dog that we never quite got the point of. Again we all laughed politely. The father did ask me if I had a favorite story. I am not the silent type and I do have many stories but none of my stories seemed to fit. My mother and I did a halting rendition of *Green Eggs and Ham* in choral speaking. That was my total contribution.

When the meal was over and we were heading out the door I realized, being the talker that I am, that I had managed to get in about six complete sentences. My friend Marilyn is more of a quiet type and I don't think she said a word the entire meal. The wife of the doctor sitting to my right didn't enter into the conversation at all. As we were being seated I asked the wife of the minister on my left where she worked and got a brief description of what she did. I never heard another word from her.

I didn't know anything about the other guests I had just met. And I didn't really know anything about the host or his family. In turn they knew nothing about me except that I am Fred and Florence's daughter.

Here was a family who seemed to have no idea how to converse, so they filled the time with nervous chatter. If they had known my father's rule, it would have been clear we didn't all get our fair share of the conversation.

It is important to have conversation as a part of every meal, both family meals and company meals. Allowing everyone time to talk is part of having a balanced conversation.

"Let's All Listen"

My father's other rule is that only one person can talk at a time. As a child I was frequently told to wait my turn as I would burst into a conversation with whatever thought had just popped into my head. Since I frequently interrupted others I thought this rule was unfair too. Now when I am at a gathering where this rule isn't followed I find I am frustrated trying to listen to several conversations at a time. I frequently find myself trying to pay attention to the person on my left when the person on my right thoughtlessly interrupts and begins talking to me. I go back and forth between conversations like a Ping-Pong ball and never really understand either person.

Another illustration of the confusion caused when common rules of courtesy aren't followed can be seen in my friend Melanie's situation. Melanie dreads going to visit her husband's family. The members of Mike's family are all talkers, and they all talk at the same time. It's not just that they have two or three conversations going on at one time but rather that all of the family members compete for *everyone's* attention. Each person tries to speak louder than the others, and no one really hears anything other than his or her own voice. Every once in awhile Mike realizes that Melanie hasn't said anything. He asks her to comment on something, and she says a sentence or two. Then the melee picks right back up again. This has happened so often that Melanie now avoids her husband's family gatherings whenever possible.

As the mother, father, host or hostess, you have the opportunity to see that everyone at the table has a chance to talk if they want to and that one person doesn't monologue the entire time. Additionally, you can direct the listening. If you are having a family meal and several people are talking and not paying attention to the main conversation, you can simply remind everyone that in your house only one person talks at a time. If you have guests and they are having separate conversations, say, "Listen, everybody, Helen has something exciting that I think you'd enjoy hearing." Your guests will get the hint and usually maintain one general conversation for the rest of the evening.

Really good conversation doesn't depend on telling everyone all you know or giving all your opinions. Grenville Kleisr has said: "Discreetly keep most of your radical opinions to yourself. When with people be a listener a large part of the time. Be considerate in every word and act, and resist the tendency to say clever things. The best evidence of your culture is the tone and temper of your conversation."

For some households, toning down the conversation and allowing each family member a chance to talk will be a challenge. For others creating meaningful conversation, or even any conversation at all, will be the area of need. A friend once told me that when she was a child, her friends didn't like to come to her house for dinner. It was because Monica's family had no conversation at the table. The children had been told to be quiet to give their father peace. But mealtimes can build positive memories through real conversation while still maintaining a peaceful atmosphere. Real conversation creates both peace and love.

Ask Interesting Questions

Being a good conversationalist boils down to two basic parts: asking interesting questions and listening. When the meal is in your home you can watch to see that each person at the table has an opportunity to share what is on his or her mind. If there is one person who seems to be left out of the conversation, ask him or her some interesting questions. Don't ask questions that can be answered with yes or no. Ask questions that allow you to get to know what is really on the other person's mind.

If conversing at the table is something new to your family you might try making it into a game. Either make up a list of numbered questions or get a little book, available in most book stores called the *Book of Questions* by Gregory Steck. This book has over 200 questions that don't have yes or no answers and they really make you think about things you may have never thought of. We suggest the *Book of Questions* in my mother's book *Raising Christians, Not Just Children*. One family told me that after reading my mother's book they had bought the *Book of Questions* and were using it every night during dinner. They made little pieces of paper and numbered them with all the questions in the book. Then they put the numbers in a little basket which they kept on the table. Each night the children would take turns picking out a number, finding that question in the book, and reading it to the family. They would take turns going around the table answering the question of the evening. They told me they have had a wonderful time getting better acquainted with their children and each other.

When I was dating I had a standard question I always asked the gentleman I was with. When there was a lull in the conversation I would ask, "In reality, if money were not a problem, what would be your idea of a fantasy vacation?" The "in reality" part eliminates ideas like going to the moon and the "if money was no problem" part lets his imagination go wild. If he thought for a moment and said, "My fantasy vacation would be to go backpacking in the Sierras, sleep under the stars, fish, and cook the fish on an open campfire" I knew I didn't need to go out with him again.

Another good question to use with someone you don't know is to ask about their jewelry. Pick an interesting piece of jewelry and say, "Tell me the story of how you got that." It may be an heirloom or it may have come from K-Mart but there is usually an interesting story that brings the person out.

Whether you are talking with your family or with guests, asking interesting questions is one part of having creative conversation around the table. Equally important is listening. Asking interesting questions will be of little value if you don't listen. James 1:19 says, "Be slow to speak, slow to anger and quick to hear." This offers the best conversation advice you could receive. I used to think if I was quiet, I was listening. Then I realized that if the person who was talking asked me a question about what they had said, I had no idea what they'd said. I suggest you be an active listener. Active listening means you respond to what the person is saying, repeat back a phrase or comment they make, and add your own thoughts to the conversation. Be involved in the conversation.

It is said that "the great gift of conversation lies less in displaying it ourselves than in drawing it out of others. He who leaves your company pleased with himself and his own cleverness is perfectly well pleased with you."

The Gift of Encouragement

To keep the meal a positive experience the conversation needs to be encouraging and uplifting. Be sure to give each person at the table a compliment before the meal is over. Save any correction or discipline for later. I was speaking on homemade memories at a women's retreat when Claire told me about mealtimes in her family. She thought the tense atmosphere and silence that was common in her household was the way everyone ate. One day she went to a friend's house for dinner. She was so surprised that everyone talked, joked with each other, and had a good time that she burst into tears. It wasn't like that at her house. She and her brother were always afraid of upsetting her father. They took the safe route and didn't say anything.

It takes extra effort to make the mealtime special but it is worth it. Set a pretty table. Use placemats or tablecloths and cloth napkins with dishes and silverware that go with the meal. Create a pleasant atmosphere by turning off the TV, turning on nice music, and limiting interruptions. Have positive and uplifting conversation which allows each person an opportunity to talk.

When the mealtime is memorable it is something you, your family, and your friends look forward to. The meal isn't just food for the body; it should also nourish the spirit and the soul.

Manners

—— ❦ ——

Chapter 6

The Double Blessing

—— ❦ ——

M any of us in the baby-boom generation have missed out on manners. We look at them as a bunch of stuffy old rules that were for our grandmothers. While many of them *are* "stuffy old rules" there are also many aspects of manners that are essential to our daily social life. I have heard manners described as the street signs of our social life. Without street signs telling us to stop, merge, or slow down, traffic wouldn't flow well and cars would be constantly involved in accidents. Likewise, manners are guidelines that allow us to function smoothly with one another. It is important for us to know basic courtesies for relating with one another.

In her book, *The Family Book of Manners*, Hermine Hartley says: "Manners are to people what polish is to silver. Manners make us shine. Manners are not a veneer you put on. They come from the heart. They are really a form of love." *The Family Book of*

Manners is an excellent book every household should have. It is written in a light, quick-reading style that doesn't labor over deep or seldom-used manners but gives a well-balanced overview of the manners that most of us need to know today. In addition it is wonderfully illustrated by Hermine's husband, Al. Al is the illustrator for the popular *Archie Comic Series* and his pictures make manners fun. Hermine covers manners as diverse as telephone manners, babysitting, and church manners.

Since *HomeMade Memories* is primarily about making the mealtime special I am going to focus on the basic table manners we need to be both polite and confident in social settings. I love how Zealandia describes manners: "It is a pity so many of us persist in regarding politeness as being merely a superficial social grace instead of what it really is, namely one of the necessities of life. Quite apart from politeness for its own sake, and as a matter of plain justice, it is invaluable as a sort of cushion or buffer to hold off the jolt that would otherwise disrupt the harmony of things." As we strive to make our homes a special place, a place where we feel safe and loved, manners and politeness offer that "cushion."

Manner Night

It is important for both adults and children to know the common courtesies of the dinner hour. While you don't want the mealtime to turn into a constant training ground, it is an excellent time to teach some of the basics. You might decide to make Monday night "manner night" and choose one basic manner to teach every week. Make a game out of showing how to place the napkin in your lap or how to hold the fork. For the rest of the week family members can simply be reminded of that week's manner! "Let's all put our napkin in our lap." At the end of the mealtime you might remind everyone of the manner you learned that day. It is important for parents to show the younger members of the family how to behave at the table by their own example. Your behavior will be more influential than your words. S. Smiles says: "Example teaches better than precept. It is the best modeler of the character of men and women. To set a lofty example is the richest bequest a man can leave behind him." In order to provide your family with a good example you need to know the basics yourself. Read over the following guidelines to be sure you know them. If you don't, learn them along with the children.

Mealtime Manners

Starting with the beginning of the meal, sit up straight and place the napkin in your lap. Wait until everyone is served before eating. In most Christian households it is also polite to wait until after the blessing has been offered. If there is a large group at the table it is generally accepted that once four or five people have been served you may begin to eat.

When you are eating be sure to hold the silverware between your thumb and forefinger rather than grabbing it with your entire hand (see diagram, p. 70). When you are cutting something on your plate, hold the food with your fork. If you are right-handed, the fork should be in your left hand. The tines of the fork should be pointing down. The knife should be in your right hand and used to gently cut through the food. Once the food is cut, set down the knife on the edge of the plate and transfer the fork to your right hand to eat. If a bite doesn't fit easily into your mouth it should be cut into smaller pieces.

Sit up straight in the chair and lift the food to your mouth. Do not lift the plate or bowl to your mouth and push the food into your mouth. Likewise, do not lean on the table and hold your head down close to the plate. It is acceptable to occasionally rest your arm or elbow on the table, but do not lean on it.

Keep your mouth closed while you are eating. It is thoughtless to expose partially chewed food to the others at the table. My mother tells me that when I was four years old a businessman came to our house for dinner. In the middle of the meal he got so involved in telling his story that he was talking with his mouth full of food. I looked over at him and said, "Don't you know you shouldn't talk with food in your mouth?" Maybe I had learned this lesson too well. If someone asks you a question and you are chewing food, rather than answer with your mouth full and risk spitting food on the table or the person next to you, simply hold up your forefinger to indicate, "Just a moment," and then finish chewing. When you have swallowed your food and are ready to respond you might want to make a light comment such as "You are just like my dentist. He sticks his hand in my mouth and then asks me a question. You waited until my mouth was full to ask me that, didn't you?" Remember to chew with your mouth closed and don't talk with your mouth full.

If something is served that you don't like, try it anyway. Do not make a negative comment that will embarrass you and the host or hostess. It is a good family policy for everyone to have at least three bites of the food that is served. This expands your family's horizons and prepares everyone for being polite in other people's homes. Children often think that anything they've never had before is bad and they declare their displeasure before they have even tried the new dish. If they must eat at least a few bites they often find they really do like it. I have been grateful my parents taught me to eat things that were not my favorite. I have been served many regional dishes I'd never seen before and hope I never see again, but I manage to eat enough to be an appreciative guest.

Don't allow the family to make negative comments about the food. When I have worked hard to make a nice dinner for Chuck and myself the last thing I want to hear is "I don't like this." Yet I do want to know if it isn't Chuck's favorite meal so I won't make it again. Chuck will tell me, "This is a nice dinner but you don't need to make it again really soon." I can take the hint without being offended.

When you have finished eating you should stay at the table until everyone is done or you have been excused. If one of the children has an excessive amount of homework to do they might be excused early but in general everyone should stay at the table through the entire meal. To indicate you have finished eating place your knife and fork in the center of the plate with the tines of the fork facing down. In your own homes place the napkin back into the napkin ring if it is appropriate. If it is dirty and needs to be replaced leave it out of the napkin ring and place it next to your plate. If you are a guest, offer to help the hostess clear the table.

With the combination of these basic table manners and an understanding of the basic table settings discussed in Chapter 4 you should be able to be comfortable and confident at most meal events, either in your own home or in a public setting. Good manners are a double blessing; they cost nothing and convey much.

Chapter 7

❦

The Happy Way

❦

Manners are important for us to use at the table, but equally important are "happy ways of doing things" when we invite guests into our home. The Bible commands us to have guests in our homes. In Titus 1:8 Paul gives guidelines for church leaders. He says, "They must enjoy having guests in their homes...." In First Peter 4:9, Peter gives the rest of us instruction on the same matter when he says, "Cheerfully share your home with those who need a meal or a place to stay for the night." And there is the famous verse in Hebrews where Paul again addresses the body of Christ and instructs us, "Don't forget to be kind to strangers, for some who have done this have entertained angels without realizing it" (13:2). With this combination of instruction and the numerous examples of hospitality shown throughout the Scriptures, I think we can conclude that inviting others into our homes for a meal or for the night is a good thing.

I have been on both sides of the fence. I have been the one opening my home both to friends and visiting missionaries, speakers, and other "strangers." And I have been the one who is the traveling speaker, the "stranger" who needs a meal or a place to stay for the night. I have been in many wonderful situations I hated to leave because I felt so loved, welcomed, and cared for; and I have been in less pleasant surroundings as well.

When we do open our home to friends or strangers for a meal or for the night there are several things we can do to reflect good "company manners" as the host or hostess. We can do things the "happy way," which leaves everyone glad the hospitality took place.

Informative Invitations

The most common form of hospitality is having friends over for dinner. When you invite those friends, neighbors, or strangers to your home use either a written or verbal invitation. Whether you invite them by mail, by telephone, or in person, be sure to let them know what kind of event you are having. If it is a couples-only gathering with just the two of you and the two of them, it is important to let your guests know that this is not the time to bring the children. If you have children yourself and you are having a couples-only meal you will, of course, need to be sure your own children are at grandma's house or visiting a friend. You might say, "I am preparing a special meal for just us grown-ups. Next time we get together we can have a barbecue for the whole family."

If the event is an open house and your guests can drop by anytime, be sure to indicate that information. When you invite people to an open house let them know what time the event is expected to be over. You might say: "We are inviting all of our friends over for a holiday open house. We will have light refreshments and would love to have you drop by anytime between 2:00 and 4:00." An open house is a great way to have people with whom you would like to get better acquainted to your home. By letting the guests know you will be serving light refreshments they will understand that this is not a meal. By giving them the ending time they know they must arrive before 4:00 and they know not to stay much longer than 4:00.

Because it has become so acceptable for people to be "fashionably late" I like to give my guests an option on their arrival time. I tell them, "I will be serving at 6:30. Please feel free to arrive anytime between 5:30 and 6:30." If you do this it is important that you be ready for them to arrive at 5:30 and that you really do serve when you say you will. On the other hand, please be aware of people's busy schedules. If you invite them to join you at 3:00 but don't intend to serve until 7:00, give your guests the option of joining you a little later.

When you invite people in person or over the telephone you usually find out right then if your guests can join you. If they need to check their calendar or check on babysitting before they can give you a firm yes or no, ask them to let you know by a certain time so that you can make your plans and do your shopping. If the invitation is by mail and it is for an open house or similar type of event you usually do not ask them to let you know if they can attend. If the invitation is for a meal, you will need to know if they are able to attend. The way to do this is to add at the bottom of the invitation either "Regrets Only," which means they only need to call you if they cannot attend, or RSVP, which is the abbreviation for the French words that mean "reply if you please." An RSVP on an invitation is a request for a response whether or not the guest can attend. I prefer the RSVP approach when I am sending a written invitation. This way I know people actually received the invitation.

Special Preparations

Once your guests respond to your invitation and you know they are coming, another "happy way" of doing things is to ask them about any food allergies or any foods they really don't like. Wouldn't you hate to have spent the time preparing a lovely meal and then find out your guests can't eat half of what you've prepared? It becomes an awkward situation for both you and the guest.

My father is very allergic to fish and recently both he and my mother were invited to a home for dinner. The hostess had not asked about any food preferences and had prepared a lovely salmon dinner. My father ate a lot of vegetables that night. The hostess felt bad she had prepared something my father could not eat. These kinds of uncomfortable situations can be avoided by simply asking if there are any foods that should not be served.

If you can relax and enjoy your own party your guests will also be more comfortable. If entertaining is new to you or if you find yourself so tired when the guests arrive that you can't enjoy them, try doing some of the preparations ahead of time. One of the things you can do is set the table after dinner the night before your party, or after breakfast the morning of the event. Seeing your beautifully prepared table will give you the comfort and encouragement you need to get everything else done.

My mother has always loved having people in her home. As a child I could never understand why my bedroom had to be spotless because she was having some friends over for dinner. Later I realized it was because she loved to tour people through the whole house. When I first started entertaining on my own I found I was wearing myself out trying to cook and have the entire house immaculate just as my mother had done. Then I discovered candles and closed doors. I still think that having company is a good excuse to give the house a good cleaning but if cleaning doesn't fit into my schedule, it is not a crisis. You too can relax when you entertain. Make sure that the main part of the house is picked up, the table is wiped down, and the guest bathroom is clean, but if you don't get to your bedroom or the kids' rooms, just close the doors. If you didn't get a chance to dust thoroughly, turn down the lights and light the candles. They will add to the ambience *and* hide the dust!

If you have invited several guests over for a sit-down dinner and they don't all know one another, it will be helpful for you to use place cards. Place cards are little cards that are often about an inch high and two inches wide. You can buy them already made at a card store or you can cut them up yourself out of index cards. On the cards you simply write the name of each person who will be in attendance. My mother-in-law gave me lovely crystal place card holders so I frequently use place cards just to get out the lovely holders. If you don't have place card holders just cut your cards so that they can be folded over and stand on their own. Once you have made up the cards spend a little time thinking about your guests. Think about who would enjoy the company of one another and arrange the place cards on the table so those who will enjoy each other will be together. Try to mix the people who know each other with some whom they do not know so that no one feels left out of the conversation.

Important Introductions

When your guests arrive you want to make them feel as comfortable as possible. If they do not all know one another, introduce them. Don't just say, "Mary, this is Bob." Try to incorporate the old journalistic W's. When you introduce someone tell the others *who* they are, *where* they are from, *what* they do, and *why* they are there. Using this approach you would introduce Bob to Mary by saying, "Mary, this is Bob Smith. Bob is a neighbor of ours; he lives just up the street. Bob works with the Federal Bureau of Investigation and he has some very interesting stories about some of the dignitaries he has worked to protect. Bob flies and loves English sports cars. I invited Bob to join us tonight because I know we will all get along wonderfully." Now when you have introduced Bob to the group you have set up many paths of conversation. The other guests may ask Bob how he met you, or they may ask about the interesting stories you alluded to, or they may ask about his flying or his cars. Be sure you know the *who, what, where,* and *why* of each of your guests so that you can give them a warm introduction to the others.

If your party is an open house, that kind of complete introduction may not be possible. In this situation give everyone a name tag and have them write how they know you under their name. Be sure to use a pen that is bold enough to be read easily. Your friends may be from church or work or from the neighborhood. This gives them a place to start a conversation with someone they don't know. Cindy, my next door neighbor, was having a surprise party for her husband, Chip. She asked me to be there to welcome and introduce the guests to one another while she was out with Chip. I gave everyone name tags and wrote their affiliation to Chip under their name. Before Chip and Cindy got home all of us who hadn't known one another previously were deep in conversation!

Putting the Pieces Together

Recently a newly married friend of mine called me for advice. She was giving her first party and had no idea what to do. I went over her plans with her. One of her biggest concerns was what to do with the people when they arrived. I told her to introduce everyone since they were coming from many different backgrounds: her work, his work, her friends, his friends, and friends from church. "Then what do I do?" she asked. I suggested she have a partially finished jigsaw puzzle on the coffee table. I had just been on a cruise where they had a puzzle table set up throughout the entire trip. It was one of the best mixers I had ever seen.

Like my friend's party, the cruise was full of people who didn't know one another. But people joined together to look for the blue pieces or the rocks. It was difficult to walk by the puzzle without trying to fit in a few pieces and before long you had made new friends. A partially finished puzzle is a good way to bring people of diverse backgrounds together. It doesn't require a lot of thought and it lets you be free to converse. In their book *Let's Make a Memory* Gloria Gaither and Shirley Dobson offer these suggestions: "When things are rushed or hectic, or there are a lot of guests in and out, set out a huge 500 piece puzzle on the coffee table or game table. Don't worry about the clutter. Just leave the puzzle out. Don't be surprised if guests who might otherwise be timid are drawn to the puzzle. Watch how many good conversations are precipitated by this simple shared task. Don't be surprised if kids are the best puzzle solvers."

What can you do if the evening has been such a success that the guests show no signs of leaving though it is getting late and you need to be up early the next day? My friend Marilyn remembers that her Uncle Henry would simply stand up, stretch, look at his watch, and say, "Well, it's 10:30." With that exclamation everyone got the hint and soon headed home. My father has been known to announce, "It's my bedtime. If you wish to stay up, feel free, but I need to get to bed." This method is equally effective. However, one of my friends inadvertently discovered a subtler way to get the job done without throwing guests out or making them feel as though they have overstayed their welcome.

Lori's husband is very security conscious. In an effort to give the house a lived-in look when they are gone he bought timers that turn the lights on and off. He hooked one up in the living room. It went on at dusk and stayed on until 10:00 P.M. They found it to be a very useful gadget even when they were home, so they used it all the time. Lori told me that one night they had company over. They were having such a good time that no one paid any attention to the time until the light went off! When they realized how late it was, the guests said they had to be leaving because they had to get up early the next day. Now Lori and her husband leave the timer on intentionally when they have company.

Chuck and I tried Lori's suggestion and found it to be a gentle reminder as well as extra security for our home. If we don't have to get up early the day after a party and we would like the fun to continue we turn the light back on and laugh off Chuck's security device. If our guests needs to leave, it gives them an opportunity to gracefully end the evening.

Special Thanks

When the evening is over you might want to send each person off with a gift or favor to remember the evening. You might have a plate of freshly baked cookies for each person or family to take home or you might have the recipes from the dinner all typed up and ready for each person. If there is a guest of honor such as a person whose birthday you have gathered together to celebrate or a visiting author or speaker, you could take a Polaroid picture of each guest with the guest of honor and let them take the picture home as a reminder of the occasion.

Emilie Barnes does a wonderful little courtesy that I have tried to adopt. I am not very good at it but I love being the recipient of Emilie's graciousness. If you are a guest at Emilie's home she sends you a thank-you note for coming. It usually arrives within a day or two while I am still intending to write her a thank-you note for inviting me. It is such a pleasant surprise to get a thank-you note from the host or hostess that I try to remember to send one to my guests. Sometimes I remember, sometimes I don't.

These company manners aren't stuffy old rules. Instead they are simply the "happy way" of doing things.

Ministry

---- ❧ ----

Chapter 8

"Angels Unaware"

---- ❧ ----

*H*omemade memories are for you, your family, and your friends. But memories can also be made with people outside your immediate circle of acquaintances. Your home gives you a wonderful opportunity to minister to people who are in need. You can set the table nicely and prepare good food for them just as you do for your family and friends.

In Romans 12:13 Paul commands us to open our homes to those in need. He says, "When God's children are in need, you be the one to help them out. And get into the habit of inviting guests home for dinner or, if they need lodging, for the night."

Sometimes we think that in order for us to have a ministry we need to set up a nonprofit organization that is tax exempt, we need to have an office and a staff. While some ministries are run that way, each of us has an opportunity for ministry in our own home. It doesn't have to be big or official. All you have to do is watch out for "God's children in need."

That person in need may be someone you see in church who is always alone. He or she may not be in financial need but may be in need of companionship or comfort. Reach out to that person, invite him or her home for dinner.

When you are willing and open to ministering to other people through your home, God will bring those who need love and nourishment into your life.

My ministry has been to single friends and neighbors. For the most part these friends have not been in a place of financial need but they have been in need of food for their soul and their spirit.

Chuck has had several friends from high school that we still see. Some have never married and some are divorced. Over the hill from us is a single guy who is one of Chuck's friends from the car club. Up the street is a single man who is a frequent guest, and across the street are two single women. My best friend from junior high school recently moved to town. A single mom that I met on our travels recently moved to our area and has begun going to our church. God seems to put single adults into our lives and I love the opportunity to minister to them. Single guys are great to feed. They love everything and compliment profusely, even if you just heat up leftovers.

While we have not personally been the ones who have led any of these single adults to the Lord, it has been exciting to watch their lives change and to be a part of that.

Don't think that if you don't make someone pray a prayer of commitment before they go home your ministry has been ineffective. Your love and the witness of your life will be a more effective ministry than pinning them down to watch evangelistic videotapes.

When Chuck and I got married and we first started having his friends from high school over, I felt uncomfortable with our Christian beliefs. Chuck had told me horror stories of their youth that had turned these men away from God and religion forever. I knew they didn't want to have any part of Christianity, but they were our friends and we invited them in anyway. At first I skipped having a blessing before the meal and we all just had a good time together. Then Chuck said, "This is our home and we say a blessing before each meal. I think when we have guests we should just do as we always do." I had been afraid of offending Chuck's friends but since this was his idea, I agreed. Saying a blessing didn't make his friends stop coming, and they quickly got the idea that they should wait for the blessing before starting to eat.

One day one of these guys stopped dropping by. I told Chuck that I thought he had fallen in love. A few months later he resurfaced. He had fallen in love with a Christian girl. He had become a Christian and they were getting married. They became so involved in church activities that we seldom saw them. We didn't lead him to the Lord but I believe that our love and subtle ministry to him made him open to dating a Christian.

Chuck's other high school friend is currently dating a girl that attends a good Christian church. He has started attending some of the activities with her. We pray for him and that positive influence in his life.

Both of these friends are ones that Chuck said wanted nothing to do with church. For over five years we have had them in our home for one event or another. We didn't hide our Christian beliefs from them, but we didn't force them on them either.

For the women across the street we have become counselors and confidants. We have helped them with their problems, shared lots of meals with them, and taken them to church. One of them had gone to church earlier in her life but hadn't really attended anywhere since she had moved to our area. She started going to church again and now her proclaimed atheist boyfriend has become a Christian. We have had both of them in our home many times. Now when we get together with them, he'll ask the blessing for the food.

Using your home as a ministry doesn't just mean bringing people to the Lord. People who are already Christian still need ministry. Carrie was new to our area and she began attending our church. Our pastor asked us all to help make Carrie and her daughter feel welcome. I have had them to our home for dinner several times. They haven't been fancy "company" meals—they have just been whatever Chuck and I were going to have for dinner that night—but our times together have ministered to Carrie's need for friendship in a new place. We have helped her get settled and given her some of the basic household items that she needed. Now that she is settled we have been to her apartment several times and have had the opportunity to encourage each other.

Ministry can take place between one Christian and another or as a way of sharing God's love with those who don't know Him.

Now you know how to create homemade memories. You know how to set the table and will soon learn to cook many elegant and easy meals. You know how to invite people in and make them feel welcome. Don't keep those memories to yourself— homemade memories are for everyone!

Menus

Chapter 9

🍎

Kitchen Basics

🍎

Any task is made easier by the availability of the right tools. Writing letters, reports, or even books is much easier with a computer or word processor. When Chuck works on his cars he always has the right equipment, and if he doesn't he goes and gets it. He says that he is not going to waste his time working with inefficient tools. So earlier in our marriage, after several meals filled with my grumbling that I didn't have the right kind of kitchen equipment, Chuck graciously offered to get me what I needed to continue producing great meals.

I started a list. Every time I came across a recipe I wanted to prepare that called for a tool or a spice I didn't have I wrote it on my list. My next birthday will long be remembered as the "kitchen birthday." First I got a big box. It was beautifully wrapped but I tore into it anyway. Inside there were lots of smaller gifts, each one individually wrapped. One package had an oven thermometer. Another had poultry shears. Another had a perfect box grater that was made of stainless steel so it wouldn't rust when I threw it into the dishwasher. Package after package was full of wonderful kitchen gadgets. I still seem to keep coming up with more things that I want for the kitchen. When a friend asked me what I wanted for Christmas this year I told her that I wanted matching, professional grade, brushed stainless steel measuring cups and measuring spoons that I could hang on the wall. At least no one thinks that I am wishy-washy!

The right tools do make cooking a pleasure and thanks to my husband, my family, and my friends, I now have a pretty complete kitchen. To help you develop a well-stocked kitchen, I have created the following collection of kitchen basics. If you stock your kitchen with the following items you will have everything you need to prepare the menus in the next chapter and most any other recipe you choose to cook.

Take an inventory of your own supplies. Use the following list and check off the items that you have already. Make a gift list of the items you need.

Kitchen supplies are great things for children to give as gifts. Many of the needed items are under five dollars and the kids will see them being used frequently. In fact, if you have children ask them to get you specific kitchen items and then have them work with you in the kitchen when you are using the item they gave you. It can be a wonderful experience when you say, "Let's go and make some cookies using that cinnamon you gave me!" And cooking is a great way to entertain energetic children.

I remember when my grandmother used to come and visit. We always wanted her to make Toll House cookies. She would tell us that we didn't need her to make them. The recipe was right on the package. We could do it ourselves now that we were grown up. But we never thought they tasted as good as when Grammie Chapman made them. When we were kids and visited her house we put on aprons and we all made Toll House cookies. Grammie Chapman lived with my sister for several years and Lauren wanted Grammie and her boys to make cookies together.

Yes, cooking together is a great bonding experience and when some of the equipment being used came from the children it makes the cooking even more fun for them!

Basic Spices and Herbs

___ Salt.

___ Pepper, whole peppercorns, and a pepper grinder. Most recipes that call for pepper will be best with freshly ground pepper. It has more flavor.

___ Nutmeg. While you can purchase grated nutmeg I suggest that you get a nutmeg grater with whole nutmegs. They are about the size of a small walnut and the entire nutmeg can be grated. It is very easy to grate and has a much fresher flavor than nutmeg that has been previously grated. If a recipe calls for freshly grated nutmeg and you only have the regular kind, use it anyway. It will still be fine.

___ Cinnamon is a versatile spice that is used in many dessert dishes. You will mostly need ground cinnamon but you may want to have some cinnamon sticks on hand. On chilly nights they are a nice touch in a cup of hot chocolate, coffee, or hot cider.

____ Ginger. For the recipes suggested in Chapter 10, ground ginger will be all you'll need. Some recipes call for fresh ginger which is a root and is found in the produce section of your grocery store rather than the spice section.

____ Whole garlic. Like ginger, whole garlic is found in the produce department. It looks like a small, lumpy onion. When a recipe asks for a clove of garlic, it means one section of the whole garlic. Once you peel off some of the dry, paperlike skin, you will see a lot of small sections. These are called cloves and they should be individually peeled before you use them. The remaining garlic will last for several months in the cupboard.

____ Garlic powder is good to have on hand for some recipes and for the times when you are out of whole garlic. It is not as good as the whole garlic but it will do in a pinch.

Garlic powder is good for making garlic toast. Just put some butter on the bread, sprinkle it with garlic powder, and broil; or wrap it in foil and heat it in the oven for 10 minutes.

____ Dry mustard is found in the spice section of your store. It is a pale yellow powder and has very different uses than what is called "prepared mustard," which is the creamy yellow condiment that we use on hot dogs and hamburgers.

—— Bay leaves are usually used whole as a decoration or in a soup or stew that will simmer for quite a while. They may be removed before serving.

Fresh Herbs

For the next grouping of herbs, I suggest you create a little herb garden that will provide you with fresh herbs year round. I have two pots of herbs. I call them my farm. One pot is outdoors and the other is in a pretty basket at my sink. Visit your local nursery to see what herbs they have available. If you have a friend who likes to cook, an attractively arranged grouping of fresh herbs would be a welcome gift. If you have the fresh herbs, use them in any recipe that calls for dried herbs. They will always give better flavor. If a recipe calls for a fresh herb but you only have the dried variety, it will usually be fine. Remember, in general dried herbs have a stronger flavor than fresh ones so use less of a dried herb than you would a fresh herb.

—— Basil
—— Marjoram
—— Thyme
—— Rosemary
—— Parsley
—— Tarragon

Basic Stock Items

In addition to herbs and spices, your cupboard should contain other ingredients that are basic to cooking. All of these items, including flour and sugar, should be kept in airtight containers to keep the little bugs out. If they do not come in airtight packaging store them in a canister or place the entire package in a zippered storage bag and seal it up tightly after each use.

___ All-purpose flour. I use the unbleached type because I've heard it's healthier. It works perfectly in every recipe that calls for all-purpose flour.

___ Whole wheat flour has a different consistency from all-purpose flour and it should only be used in recipes that are designed for it.

___ Self-rising flour has some special ingredients in it and while it is not needed often, you will encounter some recipes that call for self-rising flour.

___ Sugar. Regular white sugar is called castor sugar in British cookbooks.

___ Powdered sugar or confectioners' sugar is very white and powdery. It is used most frequently in candy and frosting and should not be used interchangeably with regular sugar.

___ Brown sugar. Unless a recipe specifically calls for dark brown sugar, light brown sugar will work in any recipe that calls for brown sugar.

___ Baking soda is also called bicarbonate of soda. Since baking soda loses its potency with age, it is best to purchase it in small boxes.

___ Baking powder is the principal leavening for quick breads such as biscuits and muffins.

___ Cornstarch is a thickening agent that is used to thicken pie and cake fillings. Some recipes call for cornstarch for thickening sauces such as gravy.

___ Molasses is a syrup made from cane sugar. It is primarily used in cakes and cookies. In the recipes in Chapter 10 you will need it for the Boston Baked Beans.

___ Honey is a sweetener that is thought to be healthier than sugar although in most cases it cannot be substituted for sugar in recipes without major adjustments to the remaining ingredients.

___ Butter Flavor Crisco. No other shortening will make as great a pie crust, and it will work for any recipe that calls for "shortening."

___ Vegetable oil can be corn oil, safflower oil, or any other basic vegetable oil. It is used in salad dressings and many cakes and breads.

___ Vegetable oil spray is great to lightly grease a pan to prevent sticking.

___ Olive oil is a lighter, more delicately flavored oil. In a pinch most recipes will work fine with vegetable oil as a substitute for olive oil.

___ Bacon fat or bacon drippings work very well as a shortening in many meat applications and will give excellent flavor to fried eggs. When you cook bacon on the stove or in the microwave, pour the bacon drippings into a small cup and store in the refrigerator. To use scoop out the needed amount.

Vinegars

Many exotic vinegars are requested in recipes and

while I do have balsamic vinegar, raspberry vinegar, tarragon vinegar, and red and white wine vinegars, I have found that if you have the following three vinegars they will cover most of your needs.

___ Distilled white vinegar is used more for cleaning than cooking but some recipes do call for "white vinegar."

___ Cider vinegar is made from apple cider and has more flavor than white vinegar but less than red wine vinegar.

___ Red wine vinegar is used in more gourmet dishes and is the vinegar used for vinegar and oil salad dressing.

Additional Items

The following additional items should be in your cupboard or pantry:

___ Vanilla is a liquid extract of the vanilla bean. It is used in many desserts and as a basic flavoring to whipped cream.

___ Almond extract is another liquid flavoring. It is typically used in very small quantities so you will need only a small bottle.

___ Burgundy or red cooking wine is used in many sauces. Cooking wine is regular wine that usually has a higher salt content to make it unpleasant to drink. If you use cooking wine you may want to use less salt than the recipe calls for. The alcohol content is burned off when the wine is cooked.

___ Nuts. You will want to keep a small variety of nuts on hand. Pecan pieces and sliced almonds will work well for most uses.

___ Unsweetened chocolate is different than cocoa. It comes in bars like a candy bar, but it is very bitter so don't try to eat it plain. Each cube or square of the bar usually equals 1 ounce.

___ Instant coffee. You may already have this in your house as a beverage. The same jar of instant coffee granules will work fine in recipes.

___ Dried minced onion flakes are called for in some recipes and they will fill in in a pinch for a small amount of fresh onion. They can be found in the spice section of your store.

___ Chicken bouillon cubes are found in the soup section of the store. Some recipes call for bouillon cubes and they are useful to keep on hand for a recipe that calls for broth or chicken stock. A bouillon cube mixed with the appropriate amount of hot water will not be as good as canned chicken broth or fresh chicken stock but it will work if you are out of both.

___ White rice, not the quick cooking kind, is used in many different recipes and is helpful to have on hand to go with leftover roasts or to stretch a meal.

Check Your Refrigerator For:

___ Butter. Try to keep a full pound of butter on hand so you'll always have enough. Margarine will work just as well as butter in most cases, although it will not have the real and rich flavor that butter has. Whether you use butter or margarine, be sure to use the stick variety not whipped or diet.

___ Eggs. Most recipes assume that you are using "large" eggs. If you buy a smaller size egg you will run the risk of damaging your results. Try to keep a full dozen on hand.

___ Milk. For cooking use only homogenized or low-fat milk. Use nonfat milk only if the recipe specifically calls for it.

___ Bacon is a staple breakfast item so I am assuming that most households will keep some on hand.

___ Prepared mustard is more commonly known as just "mustard." It is a yellow, creamy condiment and is often called for in recipes for sauces.

___ Mayonnaise and Miracle Whip can be used interchangeably. They are both used most often as a spread that is put on the insides of bread used for sandwiches.

___ Bread should be kept on hand for sandwiches and toast. Many recipes call for bread. When using bread in a recipe use a light bread such as white, sour dough, or a light type of whole wheat. For recipes, unless specified otherwise, avoid the heavy, grainy, nutty types of bread. If the bread is kept in the refrigerator it will last longer.

___ Parmesan cheese can be purchased already grated in a can or in the deli department of your grocery store as freshly grated cheese or as a wedge. The best kind to keep on hand is the grated type, either previously grated or freshly grated.

___ Unbaked pie shell. Your cooking time will be simplified if you keep a couple of unbaked pie shells in the freezer. I suggest that they be home-made and stored in an extra large zippered freezer bag.

Kitchen Tools

___ Dry-measuring cups usually come as a set made out of plastic or metal with ¼, ⅓, ½, and 1 cup sizes.

___ Liquid-measuring cups are made of clear glass (or plastic) and can be used in the oven (not the plastic ones) or microwave for things like melting butter. The newer glass ones by Pyrex with the stackable handles are easy to store. You should have 1 cup and a 2 cup measure. Each one will have various calibrations marked on the side.

___ Measuring spoons usually come in a set that includes a ¼, ½, and 1 teaspoon size, and 1 tablespoon size. Metal spoons will be the most durable and the ones with an oval-shaped bowl are easier to clean.

___ Oven thermometer is useful in letting you know when the oven is the correct temperature.

___ Portable timer is needed for keeping track of baking or roasting times. Even if you have a timer on the oven, a portable one is handy if you plan on leaving the kitchen while something is cooking.

___ Paring knife is used to trim and cut vegetables and fruit.

___ Bread knife has a scalloped edge that is specially designed to cut soft things without squashing them.

___ Chef's knives are found in several blade lengths, usually 3, 6, and 10 inches and triangular in shape. These knives are used for mincing, chopping, and peeling fruits and vegetables.

___ Slicing knives are long and narrow and are used for slicing meats.

___ Poultry shears have curved blades and one serrated edge to grip slippery poultry bones. These are needed to serve a quartered roast chicken or to cut up a whole raw chicken. They will cut right through the bones. The best ones have a spring that forces the blades back open and should be at least 10 inches long.

___ Peeler. A conventional peeler is about 6 six inches long with half of it being a metal handle and the other half the peeling blade. I always cut myself with them so I was thrilled when I discovered the Swiss or European peeler. It is about 4 inches long and has a 2-inch blade that is perpendicular to the handle rather than being an extension of it. You will find these peelers in cooking stores.

___ Apple peeler-corer-slicer. This is the most wonderful gadget. It peels, cores, and slices apples in one quick movement. It will take about 5 minutes to do enough apples for an entire pie. Without this tool peeling, coring, and slicing usually takes about 5 minutes per apple.

___ Box grater is used for grating things such as cheese and orange or lemon peels. It needs to have at least 2 sizes of grating holes: a smaller one for finely grated cheese and peels, and a larger one for cheese. The grater should be made of a good grade of stainless steel so that it can be washed in the dishwasher without rusting. It should have a handle on the top to give you a firm grip while you are grating. When grating place a piece of waxed paper down and set the grater on top of it. Grate with steady downward motions. When you are finished grating you may need to remove some of the substance from the inside of the grater with your finger or a spatula.

—— Juicer is used to obtain freshly squeezed lemon or orange juice. It can be electric or manual.

—— Meat tenderizer or mallet will have large dull spikes and is used for pounding meats to tenderize them. I recommend it mostly for pounding chicken breasts to make them thinner.

—— Nutmeg grater and nutmegs. This grater is about 5 inches long with a crescent shape. The top section has a compartment that holds 1 or 2 whole nutmegs and the lower portion has small rough-edged holes for grating. Most of the grated nutmeg will collect inside the grater. Tip the open end down and the grated nutmeg will pour out.

—— Metal tongs come in several varieties. The most common is one strip of metal that has been bent to resemble a "V" shape with teeth at each end to grip the food. Tongs are useful for turning over meat or pulling solid food out of a pot.

___ Whisks are used for lightly beating foods such as eggs.

___ Rolling pin is needed to make homemade pie crust. It should be made of wood or marble, be at least 15 inches long, and have ball bearings to allow it to roll smoothly.

___ Pastry cloth is used in making pie crust and many other pastries. It is a large sheet of thick canvaslike fabric that should be lightly coated with flour before each use.

___ Rolling pin cover is a light knit sleeve that resembles a sock. It covers most of the length of the rolling pin and helps prevent the pie crust from sticking. Like the pastry cloth, the rolling pin cover should be coated with flour before each use.

___ Pastry brush is a small tool that looks like a paintbrush and has natural, undyed bristles. The same brush may be used to baste meats or brush vegetables with butter. To clean, lay it on its side in the top rack of the dishwasher.

___ Pastry blender is needed for making pie crust and other pastry uses. It is shaped like a large "D" with a flat handle and 3 or 4 rounded blades.

___ Sifter should be used with most cake recipes and especially with those that call for it. One with a single mesh screen is sufficient and is easier to clean. It may have a crank to turn the flour and get it through the screen or it may have a squeeze handle.

___ Mixing bowls. You should have a minimum of three bowls: small, medium, and large. They may be glass or stainless steel.

— Wooden spoons should be kept right next to the stove. They are great to grab to stir sauces, soups, and stews. They should be made of close-grained hardwoods so they don't absorb the flavors or crack easily.

— Metal spoons. You'll want at least 2 different metal spoons, one that is solid to stir heavy foods and to use for serving and stuffing, and another that is slotted to allow foods to be drained.

— Metal spatula is used to lift and turn foods such as eggs and meats while they are being cooked. If your pots are Silverstone the spatula may be plastic (but this spatula is different from the rubber spatula below).

— Rubber spatulas are used to scrape the insides of bowls or pots to remove the last bit of batter or sauce. If you plan to use your rubber spatula in a hot pan be sure to get the kind that is heat resistant. The spatulas are clearly marked so it will be easy to tell which kind you have.

— Ladles should have deep bowls to keep the food from falling out and handles long enough to reach to the bottom of your pots without burning your fingers. A smaller ladle is good for pouring batter or serving gravy. The larger size is good for serving soups or stews.

— Colander or strainer. A colander is a metal bowl with holes all around the lower half of the bowl. A strainer is similar but is usually made out of a metal screen. Both are used for washing fruits and vegetables and for draining boiled foods.

___ Bulb baster. This is somewhat like a giant syringe. It has a large metal or plastic needle that is about 10 inches long and a rubber bulb at the top. It is used to baste meats while they cook. You simply insert the tip into the juices, squeeze the rubber bulb, and slowly let it go. The juices will be sucked into the needle part. Then you squeeze the bulb again to release the juices over the meat.

___ Can opener may be electric or manual. Here I'm referring to the type of can opener that goes all the way around the can and cuts the entire top piece off rather than the type that punctures a can to release liquids.

___ Corkscrew is needed to open a bottle of wine. If the only wine you ever use is cooking wine, you probably won't need a corkscrew.

Pots and Pans

It is possible to spend a great deal of money on very elaborate cookware, but to start off with the following suggestions should take care of most of your basic cooking needs. Most of the suggested stovetop pans will come in a good set of pots and pans. For the novice or casual cook I strongly suggest Silverstone pots and pans. They prevent foods from burning and sticking on the bottom.

___ Skillets or frying pans. You should have at least 2 different sizes, a smaller 6½-inch pan and a larger 10½-inch pan. They should have slightly slanted sides so you can turn the food easily.

___ Saucepans have straight sides and are deeper than frying pans. They are used for most stove-top cooking such as boiling vegetables or rice and for making sauces—hence the name saucepan. You should have at least 3 different sizes with the appropriate lids; they would be approximately 1, 2, and 3 quarts.

___ Casserole or Dutch oven is very much like a large saucepan with a lid. Saucepans have one long handle and casseroles or Dutch ovens usually have two short handles on opposite sides. They may be made from stainless steel or enamel-coated cast iron and should be between 8 and 10 quarts. The casserole or Dutch oven is used for things like Boston baked beans and spaghetti sauce.

___ Roasting pan is used for roasting meats such as baked ham, prime rib, or turkey. A good size is $17\frac{1}{2}$ x $12\frac{1}{4}$ inches with sides at least 2 inches deep. The best ones will be made of heavy stainless steel.

___ Cookie sheet or baking sheet may be coated with a nonstick finish and should be low and flat.

___ Square cake pan is used for flat cakes such as the German Apple Cake featured in the Octoberfest Dinner. It should be 8 x 8 inches with sides that are $1\frac{5}{8}$ inches deep.

___ Springform pan is used for making cheesecake and some tortes. A springform pan is circular and comes in an 8- or 9-inch diameter with removable sides to make it easier to cut and serve a cheesecake. The sides are $1\frac{1}{2}$–2 inches high.

___ Pie pans. I recommend that you have at least 2 pie pans so that you can keep at least one pie crust in the freezer. They may be glass or stainless steel and should be 9 inches in diameter.

___ Loaf pan is used for breads and loaf cakes like pound cake. The average size is about 11³/₄ x 5³/₄ x 3¹/₂ inches.

___ Cake pans are used for making layer cakes such as a traditional birthday cake. They are usually made of stainless steel or tin and are 8 inches in diameter.

___ Casserole dishes are usually made of glass or ceramic. A set of 3 in small, medium, and large sizes will equip you for most needs. They are used for making casseroles and dishes like scalloped potatoes.

___ Muffin tin. While the recipes in Chapter 10 do not call for a muffin tin, it is a basic item that should be in a well-equipped kitchen. A 6- or 12-holed tin will be sufficient.

___ Microwave vegetable steamer. To some this might seem like an odd requirement, but once you get used to using one you'll wonder why you ever cooked vegetables any other way. Rubbermaid makes a very good one. It has 3 parts, a solid bottom bowl, another bowl that fits inside the bottom bowl and has little slots in the bottom, and a clear plastic lid.

___ Microwave bacon cooker. This item has a grill-like surface that allows the grease to drip away from the bacon.

Electric Appliances

I am not a huge fan of electric appliances just because I don't like the clutter on the counter but I consider this list to be the minimum.

—— Microwave oven is pretty much of a standard in most homes today. If you don't already have one, I suggest getting one of the new combination units like Express Meals from Sunbeam. It is a microwave, regular oven, toaster, and broiler all in one. It eliminates having another toaster on the counter and offers extra oven space when you need to cook two items at different temperatures at the same time.

—— Food processor is a very useful item for chopping, slicing, or grating a large quantity of fruit, vegetables, or cheese. Most food processor parts can easily be washed in the dishwasher. I have this funny old food processor that any real gourmet would turn his or her nose up at. I love the one I have because it allows me to use both the chopper blade and the slicing/grating blade at the same time. If you don't already have one you might look for one with that feature. I find it especially helpful for my cheesecake recipe. (The only one I know of that has this feature is made by Black and Decker.)

—— Electric mixer does not need to be a big expensive unit with a base and a stand. A strong portable one will work for most normal uses. Most come with at least 3 speeds.

—— Blender will have several speeds and have a glass or plastic container that can be washed in the dishwasher. It is useful for blending thin batters like Yorkshire pudding batter.

Odds and Ends

A few remaining items are needed to fully equip you for efficient use of your kitchen:

____ Toothpicks are used to test whether or not a cake is done. They are also good to close up the opening of stuffed poultry.

____ Potholders. You should have at least 2 thick potholders to allow you to remove hot pans from the oven.

____ Paper towels are good for all kinds of cleaning. In cooking you may need them to absorb the excess grease from bacon or to line a salad bowl to absorb the water from the lettuce. Remove the paper towels before tossing the salad and serving.

____ Aluminum foil will work as a lid for a pot or pan that doesn't have one and is good for covering any item that needs to be covered during cooking.

____ Wax paper is helpful to have to place under the box grater while grating. The fine bits of grated food can easily be combined with the other ingredients by picking up the waxed paper and pouring the grated food.

____ Plastic wrap makes an airtight cover for bowls and food items.

There are many other items that you may find useful in creating an organized kitchen. But if you have these basic items you will be well equipped for all the recipes in the following chapter and almost any other recipe you choose to prepare.

---- ❦ ----

Chapter 10

Creative Cooking

---- ❦ ----

I love to cook but I don't love to labor in the kitchen. I like to produce meals that impress my friends and family with a minimal amount of work. Since I have found many men and women with similar interests I have included a special selection of recipes that are creative and impressive without being so difficult or tedious that you will pledge never to cook again. All of the recipes are arranged into complete menus. If you are a gifted gourmet you may want to skip some of the sections or you may want to add some additional items of your own. But if you are new to cooking or are afraid to entertain because you aren't sure how to make everything come out at the same time, or if you don't know what to put with what, you will find this section very helpful in creating homemade memories.

As I have taught friends to cook and helped others plan parties I have observed where their biggest fears lie and I have designed the Creative Cooking section of *HomeMade Memories* to ease those concerns. You will notice each menu is divided into several sections.

First there is a story of introduction to give you a feel for the type of meal to expect and the type of table settings that would be appropriate. The stories tell my personal background reasons for including the menu. There were so many wonderful recipes I had a tough time deciding which ones to include. I hope you will be happy with my choices.

Next you will find a preparation timetable. The first time you make any of these recipes I suggest that you follow the timetable exactly. I have tested the timing of each menu and have spelled out what you should do and when, so that everything is ready at the same time. If your cooking time is interrupted by the needs of little ones, you'll need to build some extra time into the proposed schedule. If you have older children in your home, you can make your preparation even easier by enlisting their help. Some of the menus can be ready from start to finish in 15 minutes and others are stretched out over a day or two. Some may be time-consuming but none are so difficult that you'll want to give up. One of the basic premises of my style of cooking is "there should not be more than one difficult recipe per menu."

After the Timetable there is a complete shopping list for you to review and use to check your cupboards before you begin to cook. I have been known to go to the store or borrow from the neighbors three different times for one meal. If you are like me you will find the Shopping List to be extremely helpful.

The Shopping List is divided into two sections, Stock Items and Special Purchases. If you have followed the suggestions in Chapter 9, "Kitchen Basics," you should have all the stock items on hand. However, it is a good idea to check them anyway before going to the store. Rather than list the exact amount of cups or teaspoons of an item you will need, I have usually listed just the item. To be sure that you have a good stock of that item on hand, try to keep full packages of stock items. If butter or eggs are listed be sure you have a full pound of butter and a full dozen eggs on hand. If the shopping list includes flour be sure to have a full or nearly full bag.

The Special Purchases section of the Shopping List includes the items that you probably don't keep on hand such as the meat, fruit, or vegetables that are needed for that menu. If the items come in a package or a carton, such as hot dogs or milk, they are listed without a quantity. If the items are available individually without having to buy an entire package, such as onions or tomatoes, the exact quantity will be listed. Be sure to check both the Stock Items and Special Purchases before you begin to cook.

At the end of each menu is a special section titled "Kids' Helps." This section offers suggestions on ways that children from five to ten years old can help with the meal preparation. Cooking together is a wonderful way to both entertain the kids and teach them to cook.

Each menu is carefully planned to include the basic food groups. Every one has a meat or main dish, a vegetable, and a starch. The different recipes have been chosen for several reasons. One is that the combination of recipes will complement each other nicely. My father always taught me to never have two items of the same color and the same consistency on the same plate. So each menu is planned with a variety of colors and textures. You won't find meat loaf with mashed potatoes and creamed corn. They are too much the same consistency, all soft and mushy; and they are too much the same color, all beigy. Instead you will find meat loaf with scalloped potatoes and a colorful mixed-vegetable combination of green, yellow, and red with apple pie and ice cream to finish it off! Since appearance plays a large part in a meal's appeal, each of these menus is designed to look appetizing on the plate.

In addition to the appearance and texture of the foods together, their tastes are also compatible. There are not too many sweet things or too many rich things in one meal. Some of the menus are specially designed to be light and others, such as the Thanksgiving Dinner, are traditionally designed to make you feel fat and happy!

The recipes have also been chosen to go with one another because their work load is compatible. Most of these recipes are incredibly easy. If there is one that is more difficult it will have complete instructions that spell out every step and it will be combined with other recipes that are easy, so the total menu won't be overwhelming. As you create your own menus, keep in mind "only one difficult recipe per menu."

Another interesting feature of these menus is that none of them have any fussy food. My sister is a real gourmet cook while I am just a pretend gourmet cook. She'll spend hours precisely measuring and preparing an elegant meal that includes some kind of wild mushrooms and baby vegetables. I like to make foods that look and taste great and are a little unusual but I don't like to cook things that will fail if my dash of salt is different than the one the cook who wrote the recipe had in mind. I also don't like using a lot of strange ingredients that I have to chase all over town to find. My sister Lauren, the gourmet cook, told me once that my souffle wouldn't rise if I didn't measure every item exactly, so I've never made a proper souffle.

If every measurement has to be exact, cooking takes on a quality that is much like work. When cooking becomes like work it is no fun. So every one of these recipes allows for some flexibility. When you measure one cup of flour you don't have to flatten out the top of the measuring cup before adding the flour to the other ingredients. Just fill the measuring cup and empty the flour in. With all the spices, if you use a little more or a little less than the recipe calls for the world won't come to an end. I have included exact measurements of each spice for those of you that are new to cooking or for those who can't stand to do things haphazardly.

If you are new to cooking I suggest that in the beginning you follow the exact measurements. When you measure out a tablespoon of sugar, for example, pour it into your cupped hand so you can begin to get a feel for how much a tablespoon is. Once you have a sense for the way a half-teaspoon feels in your hand, you can skip the measuring spoons altogether. Don't get so careless that you abandon the recipe completely but if you use a pinch of salt instead of a dash or ½ teaspoon of cinnamon instead of ¼, you won't ruin any of these meals.

While none of these menus are exactly "health food," as you will notice by the free use of sugar, butter, and meats, they are all full of fresh, whole ingredients and that makes them healthier than some "health food." I eat this kind of "health food" almost every day and I recently had my cholesterol checked. I came out with very low cholesterol, "almost too low," the doctor said. Except for the Twinkies in the English Trifle, you will find virtually no pre-packaged foods. This cuts out almost all chemical preservatives and artificial flavors or colors. The recommended cooking time for the fresh vegetables leaves them cooked but crisp and full of their natural nutritional values. Almost every menu has either fresh vegetables or fresh fruit and therefore a salad isn't needed. If you like a lot of salad, feel free to add a crisp green salad to any of the suggested menus except the Christmas Dinner menu, which has its own special salad.

There are menus that are quick and menus that are creative. Some are full of Americana delights and others will broaden your culinary horizons. Easter, Thanksgiving, and Christmas are all traditional times for creating homemade memories so I have included a complete menu for each of the major holidays. You will find many menus and lots of ideas for creative cooking in this section because homemade memories require homemade food.

After Work Company Dinner

Spinach Balls with
Mustard Sauce
Apricot Game Hens
Double Orange Carrots
Littauer's Famous Cheesecake

Serves 6

When we invite company in for dinner, most of us want to have something special, something that will impress our guests. This menu does just that. It is a meal that is different from what most people eat every day and that makes it special. There is an entire Cornish game hen for each person. The Apricot Game Hens look almost regal as they sit proudly on each plate. Stuffing is used instead of potatoes or rice to provide the starch for the meal, and the Double Orange Carrots offer a very different vegetable that is really quick and easy.

What better way to end an impressive company dinner than with a homemade cheesecake. Almost no one makes fresh cheesecake because they think it is too much work. Gourmet cheesecake shops charge $20 or more for one that isn't as good as this one. You don't need to let anyone know how easy it really is. The actual work of preparing the cheesecake won't take you more than about 15 minutes. It does need to be made at least a day ahead and then it will need to cook for an hour, but it can be put together quickly. I have been known to make one at night before bedtime. I put it in the oven and go to bed with the alarm set for one hour later. When the alarm rings I drag my body out of bed, get the cheesecake out of the oven, put it in the refrigerator, and go back to bed.

In fact, recently that is exactly what I did. I was having my husband's boss and his wife, a psychiatrist who is head of a major hospital and his wife, my friends Glen and Marilyn Heavilin, and my parents over for dinner—a whole group of people who are involved in speaking, writing, and counseling. The only night that we could all get together was a weeknight so that was when we did it.

I got home at 5:30 and my guests were due between 7:00 and 7:30. I had made the cheesecake the night before so it was all ready. In the morning before work I made the Spinach Balls and put them in the freezer and did the starting preparation for the Mustard Sauce. When I got home all I had to do was to prepare the Apricot Game Hens, set the table, and fix the carrots, in that order. When my guests arrived I was all cleaned up and ready for them. If you follow the timetable you can have a formal company dinner after work and be relaxed enough to enjoy it.

Timetable

1–3 nights before serving:
Prepare and bake Cheesecake.
Prepare and freeze Spinach Balls.

The morning before serving:

Combine dry mustard and vinegar for Mustard Sauce.

Prepare Spinach Balls and freeze if this has not already been done.

1½ hours before serving:

Prepare apricot sauce.

Prepare stuffing.

1¼ hours before serving:

Prepare Apricot Game Hens.

1 hour before serving:

Cook Game Hens.

Cook Spinach Balls.

Prepare Double Orange Carrots.

45 minutes before serving:

Cook Mustard Sauce.

30 minutes before serving:

Bake the Spinach Balls.

10 minutes before serving:

Cook Double Orange Carrots.

Shopping List

Stock Items

___ Butter (four sticks)	___ Nuts
___ Sugar	___ Vanilla

___ Dry mustard   ___ Vinegar
___ Nutmeg   ___ Wine vinegar
___ Salt and pepper   ___ Eggs

Special Purchases

___ 1 package graham crackers (approximately 12)
___ 4 8-ounce packages cream cheese
___ ½ lemon
___ 1 16-ounce container sour cream
___ 2 10-ounce packages frozen chopped spinach
___ 3 6-ounce packages stuffing mix
___ 1 5-ounce wedge Parmesan cheese
___ 4 small green onions
___ 1 jar apricot-pineapple preserves
___ White wine or white grape juice
___ ¾ cup chopped pecans
___ 6 Cornish game hens
___ 1 medium onion
___ 1 pound carrots
___ 4 ounces dried apricots

🐚 Littauer's Famous Cheesecake 🐚

Preheat oven to 350 degrees.

Crust

1 package graham crackers (approximately 12)
1 stick butter
A handful of nuts (pecans or walnuts work especially
    well)

In the food processor chop up the nuts and leave them in the food processor. Using the grater blade, press the crackers into the bowl of the food processor and do the same with the butter. (If your machine allows you to use both the chopper blade and the grater blade at the same time, leave them both on through the entire process.) Use the chopper blade to mix all the ingredients. Empty the contents into the cheesecake pan and press into the bottom and up the sides about 2 inches. Set aside. It is not necessary to wash the food processor bowl before the next step.

Filling

4 8-ounce packages cream cheese
4 eggs
1 cup sugar
Juice of ½ lemon
2 teaspoons vanilla

Using the chopper blade, blend all ingredients except the cream cheese in the bowl of the food processor. Using the grater blade, press the cream cheese into the mixture. Using the chopper blade, blend all the ingredients together until they are smooth. Pour the filling into the crust and bake for 1 hour (until a toothpick inserted in the center comes out clean).

Topping

1 16-ounce carton sour cream
¼ cup sugar
½ teaspoon vanilla

While the cake is cooking, mix all the topping ingredients in the food processor; again, no need to wash the bowl. When the cake is done, pour on topping and bake for another 5 minutes. Remove cake from oven and refrigerate.

This cheesecake is best when made at least 24 hours before serving but will be even better if it is made 2–3 days ahead. It will serve about 10. It's also excellent topped with fresh fruit.

❦ *Spinach Balls with Mustard Sauce* ❦

Mustard Sauce

Prepare at least 4 hours before serving (may be prepared as much as 8 hours before serving).

1 regular-size jar dry mustard, 1.75 ounces
½ cup white vinegar

Combine the mustard and vinegar in a small dish with a lid.

Cover and shake to blend. Let this mixture stand in a covered dish 4–8 hours.

¼ cup sugar
1 egg yolk

In a small saucepan, mix the sugar and the egg yolk. Add the mustard-vinegar mixture and cook over low heat, stirring constantly until the mixture thickens slightly. Pour back into covered dish, cover, and chill until ready to serve. The sauce may be served warm, cool, or room temperature.

You may want to warn your guests that this sauce will really clear their sinuses.

Spinach Balls

Preheat oven to 350 degrees.

May be prepared 3–4 days ahead and frozen until ready to cook.

2 10-ounce packages frozen chopped spinach, thawed and squeezed dry
1 6-ounce package stuffing mix
1 5-ounce wedge Parmesan cheese, grated
1 stick butter, melted
4 small green onions, white and light green part only
3 eggs
A dash of freshly grated nutmeg

Thinly slice the green onions. Combine the green onions and all the other ingredients in a large bowl and mix well. The ingredients will mix most easily if they are mixed with your hands. Using your hands, roll the mixture into 1-inch balls and place on a cookie sheet. (If the Spinach Balls are being frozen, cover them with foil or plastic wrap and freeze at this point.) Bake the Spinach Balls in a 350-degree oven until golden brown, 10–15 minutes. Serve warm with the Mustard Sauce for dipping.

❦ *Apricot Game Hens* ❦

Preheat the oven to 350 degrees.

Sauce

1 cup apricot-pineapple preserves
⅓ cup white wine or white grape juice
½ stick butter

Combine preserves, wine or grape juice, and butter in a small saucepan and bring to a boil over medium heat, stirring frequently. Set aside.

Game Hens

2 6-ounce packages of Stove Top San Francisco Style (or similar) stuffing mix, made according to package instructions
A handful of chopped pecans
6 Cornish game hens, thawed, inside pieces removed and rinsed

Prepare stuffing mix according to package directions. Add the pecans and stir to blend.

Sprinkle hens inside and out with salt and pepper. Loosely fill the cavity with stuffing. Do not pack the stuffing inside or overfill. Secure the opening by overlapping the pieces of skin and pinning with a toothpick. Arrange the hens in a roasting pan, keeping them from touching each other. Heavily coat each hen with the glaze. Bake the hens at 350 degrees for 1 hour. Recoat the hens with sauce every 15 minutes until the sauce is all used up. Once the sauce is used, continue basting the hens with pan juices.

Place remaining stuffing mix in a baking dish and bake along with the hens.

To serve, place some of the extra stuffing on the plate and set the hen next to it. Just before serving, spoon some of the sauce from the bottom of the roasting pan over the hen.

❦ *Double Orange Carrots* ❦

5 tablespoons butter
1 medium onion
1 pound carrots
4 ounces dried apricots
½ cup chicken broth
2 teaspoons red wine vinegar
salt and freshly ground pepper

Slice the onion in the food processor. Melt the butter in a large frying pan over medium-high heat. Add the sliced onion and cook until the onion is lightly browned. Meanwhile, in the food processor, shred the carrots. Slice the apricots into thin strips like matchsticks. Add the carrots and apricots to the onions and cook 2 minutes, stirring frequently. Stir in the chicken broth, cover and cook until the carrots are crisp-tender, about 5 minutes.

Uncover and continue cooking until all the liquid evaporates. Sprinkle with the wine vinegar, salt, and pepper. Serve.

Kids' Helps

Cheesecake crust: Have the children push the graham crackers and butter through the food processor. They can empty the contents of the food processor into the cheesecake pan.

Cheesecake filling: If the children are old enough to crack open eggs, they can add the eggs to the food processor bowl, measure the sugar, and add the sugar to the bowl. They can press the cream cheese through the food processor. While the bowl will be too heavy for young children to pour, they can use a spatula to help scrape the remnants from the bowl.

Mustard Sauce: Once you have separated the egg, a child can place the egg yolk in the pan and add the sugar. Once the vinegar/mustard mixture has been added, a child can stand on a step stool and stir the sauce until it thickens.

Spinach Balls: Children will love to help with this recipe. Allow them to open the stuffing packages and pour them into the bowl. They can add the grated cheese, pour in the melted butter, add the chopped onions, and (if they are able) crack open and add the eggs. Once all the ingredients have been added, let the kids stick their clean hands in and squeeze and squish the mixture until the ingredients are blended.

Apricot Game Hens (sauce)*:* Children can spoon the preserves into the pan, add the wine or grape juice, and unwrap and add the butter. They can stand on a step stool and stir the sauce until it comes to a boil.

Apricot Game Hens: Allow the children to spoon the sauce over each hen. If they are old enough to be near a hot oven they can spoon more sauce over each hen during the cooking time. As with every activity involving the stove or oven, this should be done only with supervision.

Double Orange Carrots: Children can press the onion through the food processor and then do the same with the carrots. They can stir the carrots, onions, and apricots while they cook.

🍎 World's Quickest Dinner 🍎

Orange Chicken and Rice
Ice Cream Sundaes

Serves 4

While it is wonderful to take a Sunday afternoon and prepare a great meal that fills the entire house with a fragrance that makes your mouth water, sometimes we need fast food. But fast food doesn't have to mean junk food.

This menu has the trademarks of my cooking: whole, fresh ingredients; a variety of color, texture, and flavor; and simple preparation. But this entire meal takes only 15 minutes to prepare. You can't go out for "fast food" in that short a time.

This meal has an elegant touch to it so set an elegant table. Setting out the good dishes doesn't take any longer than setting out the everyday plates. Use a tablecloth or lace placemats with nice cloth napkins. Put out the stemmed glasses and light the candles while the dinner cooks.

Next time you need fast food, pick up the 6 special purchase ingredients and make your own. Just because it is fast, doesn't mean it can't be festive!

Timetable

15 minutes before serving:
Start cooking the rice.
Cut up the chicken and carrots.

10 minutes before serving:
Heat the frying pan and melt the butter.

8 minutes before serving:
Cook the chicken and carrots.

Shopping List

Stock Items

___ White rice, not the quick-cooking kind
___ Pepper
___ Dried rosemary
___ Flour
___ Salt
___ Butter
___ Fresh parsley

Special Purchases

___ 2 boneless chicken breasts, 4 pieces
___ 2 medium carrots
___ 1 lemon
___ 1 orange
___ Vanilla ice cream
___ Hot fudge sauce

❦ *Orange Chicken and Rice* ❦

Serves 4
(Can easily be doubled)

2 cups white rice, cooked according to package
    directions
½ cup flour
1 teaspoon salt
½ teaspoon freshly ground pepper
2 boneless chicken breasts (usually purchased in
    half-breast pieces, 2 breasts would be 4 pieces)
1 stick butter
2 medium carrots
Juice of ½ lemon
Juice of ½ orange
2 teaspoons dried, crumbled rosemary
2 tablespoons minced fresh parsley

Skin the chicken breast and cut into bite-size pieces.
Trim the carrots and cut into 2-inch long julienne
pieces (the carrots should look like thick matchsticks).

In a plastic bag, combine the flour, salt, and freshly
ground pepper. Add the chicken pieces, twist the bag
closed, and shake until the chicken is well coated
with the flour mixture.

In a large frying pan, melt the butter over medium
heat and then add the chicken and carrot pieces.
Increase the temperature to medium-high and cook
the chicken and carrots 3–5 minutes, stirring frequently. Add the juices and rosemary and cook an
additional 2 minutes or until the liquids thicken and

make a nice sauce. Divide the chicken and sauce into 4 portions and serve over the rice. Top with the fresh minced parsley.

For dessert serve a good quality vanilla ice cream topped with prepared hot fudge sauce.

Kids' Helps

Orange Chicken Rice: Kids will love to shake the plastic bag with the chicken pieces and flour. Be sure the bag is twisted tightly shut before giving it to them. They can also stir the chicken and carrots as they cook.

Sherried Chicken Dinner

Sherried Chicken with Wild Rice
Asparagus with Lemon Butter
Easy Chocolate Mousse

Serves 4

This dinner has a gourmet flair that is very impressive, yet it is simple and quick to prepare. Because of this it is a favorite of mine for weeknight entertaining or a romantic dinner with Chuck. It is a unique dish but its ingredients are not so odd that no one will want to eat them. Chicken is a normal item but the sherry sauce makes it special. Everyone has rice at one time or another, but wild rice has a unique nutlike flavor. We know that we need to eat our vegetables and asparagus in a light lemon butter is a perfect balance for this lovely meal. We all love chocolate but somehow when chocolate pudding is upgraded to chocolate mousse it becomes a gourmet dessert. All this in 60 minutes from start to finish, including setting the table and getting yourself ready.

The actual menu is planned to serve four people but if you choose to have a candlelit dinner for two the recipes can be easily cut in half. For the Chocolate Mousse, I recommend that you make the full recipe anyway since it will keep nicely for several days in the refrigerator if it is well covered with plastic. It will be great for lunch or dinner the next night.

Since this dinner has an elegant flavor, I suggest that you serve it in a formal setting. While the rice is cooking set the table with your best settings and then go freshen yourself up for a quiet, relaxed romantic evening for just the two of you or to share with another couple.

Try it. You will see that the Sherried Chicken Dinner will become a favorite of your friends and family too.

Timetable

1 hour before serving:

Prepare the Chocolate Mousse.

45 minutes before serving:

Prepare the wild rice according to package instructions. Be sure to check the package; some brands may recommend a little longer cooking time.

15 minutes before serving:

Clean and prepare asparagus.
Skin the chicken and coat with the flour.

10 minutes before serving:

Cook the chicken.
Cook the asparagus.

Shopping List

Stock Items

___ Butter   ___ Eggs

___ Salt   ___ Pepper
___ Flour   ___ Vanilla
___ Fresh parsley

Special Purchases

___ Wild rice
___ 1 pound boneless chicken breasts
___ 1 pound asparagus
___ 1 lemon
___ Sherry
___ 1 12-ounce package chocolate chips
___ 2 large cartons whipping cream

🦃 Sherried Chicken 🦃

Wild rice, prepared according to package instruc-
    tions. (To give the rice a little more flavor add a
    chicken bouillon cube to the boiling water and
    cook as directed.)
2 boneless chicken breasts, approximately 1 pound
2 teaspoons salt
1 teaspoon pepper
4 tablespoons flour
¾ stick butter
½ cup regular or cooking sherry
½ cup fresh minced parsley

Pull the skin off the chicken breasts and pound them
with a meat mallet to a thickness of about ¼ inch.
Combine the flour, salt, and pepper in a plastic bag
and coat the chicken pieces with the mixture by

placing them in the bag one at a time, twisting the bag closed, and shaking it gently.

In a large frying pan, melt the butter over medium-high heat. Add the chicken pieces and cook 4–5 minutes on each side.

Add the sherry and boil for 1 minute or until it thickens slightly.

Serve on the plate with a little of the chicken overlapping the wild rice.

❧ *Asparagus with Lemon Butter* ❧

1 pound fresh asparagus
Juice of ½ lemon
1 tablespoon butter

Clean the asparagus. Remove the tough ends one at a time by holding one end of the asparagus in each hand and bending it until it snaps. It will break off right where the tough part ends and the tender part begins.

Place a couple of tablespoons of water in the bottom portion of a microwave steamer. Place the asparagus in the top portion, cover and microwave on high 6–8 minutes, until the asparagus stalks are tender but not mushy. They should retain their fresh green color.

Empty the water from the bottom of the steamer and place the cooked asparagus in the bottom portion.

Add the lemon juice and the butter. Cover and shake gently to coat the asparagus with the lemon butter.

To serve, gently remove the asparagus with tongs, place on the plates, and pour any remaining lemon butter over the asparagus.

❦ *Easy Chocolate Mousse* ❦

1 12-ounce package of chocolate chips (2 cups)
1½ teaspoons vanilla
A pinch of salt
1½ cups whipping cream
6 egg yolks
3 egg whites
Whipped cream for topping

In a small saucepan, heat the 1½ cups of whipping cream just to the point of boiling. Set aside.

Using the food processor with the chopper blade attachment, combine the chocolate, vanilla, and salt using several on-off turns. Add the hot cream and continue mixing until the chocolate is completely melted, about 30 seconds. Add the egg yolks and mix an additional 5 seconds to blend them into the chocolate mixture. Transfer the mixture to a bowl and set it aside.

Using an electric beater, beat the egg whites in a small bowl until they form stiff peaks. Gently fold the egg whites into the chocolate mixture. (Folding is a very gentle type of stirring that mixes ingredients without losing the fluffiness of the egg whites. To do it, hold a large spoon almost sideways and gently pull it across the bottom of the bowl and over the top in a circular motion.) Once the mixture has an even color, pour it into 4 dessert dishes and chill. Before serving, top the mousse with whipped cream.

Kids' Helps

Sherried Chicken: Once the chicken breasts have been skinned, allow the older children to pound them. They will enjoy shaking up the chicken pieces in the plastic bag with the flour and spices, and they can turn the chicken breasts when they are ready to be turned.

Asparagus with Lemon Butter: Show the children how to trim the asparagus, and then let them snap off the tough ends themselves.

Easy Chocolate Mousse: Turning the food processor on and off is great fun for kids, so let them do it. They can also hold the beater while the eggs whites are beating and if you show them how to fold in the egg whites, they can carefully blend the chocolate and egg whites together.

Late Night Soup Supper

Corn Chowder
Grilled Cheese Sandwiches
Brownie Cookies

One of my very favorite meals from childhood is this simple soup supper made of Corn Chowder and Grilled Cheese Sandwiches. I regularly get cravings for it and although it is not Chuck's favorite, he has learned to like it also. I come home from work and make a big pot of Corn Chowder. Chuck happily eats one meal and then I take it to work and share it with my employees. It always tastes better the next day anyway.

To top off this simple supper, I suggest these fabulous Brownie Cookies. They are a perfect finish and they also store well.

Serve this hearty meal in heavier stoneware bowls set on large plates with the sandwiches cut in halves on the plate. Set the table with casual placemats and napkins, and a soup spoon is all that is needed.

Timetable

1 hour before serving:
Prepare and cook the Corn Chowder, minus the potatoes.

45 minutes before serving:

Peel, cut, and boil the potatoes.
Prepare Brownie Cookies.
Preheat the oven to 350 degrees.

20 minutes before serving:

Place Brownie Cookies in preheated oven.
Drain the potatoes and add them to the Corn
    Chowder.
Prepare Grilled Cheese Sandwiches.

10 minutes before serving:

Cook Grilled Cheese Sandwiches.

5 minutes before serving:

Turn Grilled Cheese Sandwiches.
Remove the Brownie Cookies from the oven.

1 minute before serving:

Place Brownie Cookies on a cooling rack.

Shopping List

Stock Items

___ Bacon
___ Pepper
___ Tarragon
___ Mayonnaise or
    Miracle Whip
___ Unsweetened chocolate
___ Butter

___ Milk
___ Parsley
___ Bread
___ Vegetable oil spray
___ Salt
___ Sugar
___ Eggs

___ Instant coffee   ___ Vanilla
    granules   ___ Flour

Special Purchases

___ 1 medium onion
___ 2 cans cream-style corn
___ 2 cans niblet corn
___ 6 small red potatoes
___ Sliced cheddar cheese
___ 1 12-ounce package chocolate chips
___ 1 package nut pieces

🐾 *Corn Chowder* 🐾

6 slices bacon, cut into ¼-inch pieces
1 medium onion, chopped
2 cans cream-style corn
2 cans niblet corn, drained
4 cups milk
1 teaspoon salt
1 teaspoon pepper
2 teaspoons parsley
1 teaspoon tarragon
6 small red potatoes

In a large pot, cook the bacon over medium heat until it just begins to get limp. Add the chopped onion and cook until the bacon is lightly browned and the onion is slightly transparent. Add the corns, the milk, and the seasoning. Reduce heat to medium-low and simmer for 1 hour, stirring occasionally.

Meanwhile, peel the potatoes and cut them into bite-size pieces. Bring a medium saucepan of water to a boil. Add the potatoes and boil for about 10 minutes or until they are just tender. You don't want them to be mushy. Once the potatoes are cooked, drain the water and add them to the Corn Chowder. Continue simmering for the remainder of the hour's cooking time.

❦ Grilled Cheese Sandwiches ❦

2 slices bread for each person being served
2 slices cheddar cheese for each sandwich
Mayonnaise or Miracle Whip
Sweet pickle relish
Vegetable oil spray, such as Pam

Using a knife, spread a thin layer of mayonnaise or Miracle Whip on the inside of each piece of bread. On one piece of bread for each sandwich, spread a thin layer of relish. Place the 2 slices of cheese on top of the piece of bread with the relish and arrange them in such a way that all corners of the bread have some cheese on them. Place the other piece of bread on top of the cheese, mayonnaise-side down.

Heat a griddle or frying pan to medium. Spray lightly with the vegetable oil. Cook the Grilled Cheese Sandwiches about 5 minutes on each side or until the bread is nicely toasted and has a golden color and the cheese is melted.

To serve, cut sandwiches in half from corner to corner (giving you 2 triangular pieces) and place on plate.

❦ *Brownie Cookies* ❦

Preheat the oven to 350 degrees.

5 ounces unsweetened chocolate, broken into pieces
1⅓ cups sugar
1 stick butter, room temperature
2 large eggs
1 tablespoon instant coffee granules
1 tablespoon vanilla
1 cup flour
1 12-ounce package chocolate chips
¾ cup chopped nuts; walnuts, or pecans
¼ teaspoon salt
Vegetable oil spray, such as Pam

Spray 2 cookie sheets with vegetable oil.

Using the food processor with the chopping blade in place, combine the unsweetened chocolate and sugar until well blended, about 2 minutes. The chocolate will be almost as fine as the sugar with no large chunks left.

Add the butter, eggs, coffee, and vanilla and blend using the chopping blade until they all have a smooth and fluffy consistency.

Add the chocolate chips, nuts, and salt. Blend in lightly by using 2 or 3 short on-off turns.

Using a soup or serving-size spoon, drop cookie batter on the prepared cookie sheets by the spoonful. Be sure to leave at least one inch between each cookie. Bake in the preheated 350-degree oven for about 10 minutes or until the cookie tops look dry and are still slightly soft to the touch. Remove from oven and cool on cookie sheet for 5 minutes. Then, using a spatula, lift cookies off the cookie sheet and place them on a cooling rack. Once they are cooled they can be served right away or stored in an airtight container for up to 4 days.

Kids' Helps

Corn Chowder: Once the bacon and onion are cut, let the children add them to the pot and stir them while they cook. Open the cans of corn and let them add the corn and milk to the pot and stir them to blend.

Grilled Cheese Sandwiches: Children can spread the mayonnaise and relish on the bread, although you may need to supervise the quantity. They can also put the cheese on the bread.

Brownie Cookies: Kids can help with all the food processor uses by turning the machine off and on when you tell them to. They can also add most of the ingredients with your help. Let them spoon the dough onto the pan. Of course they'll love to lick the spoon and scrape the remaining chocolate from the processor bowl!

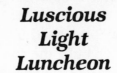

Luscious Light Luncheon

**Light Lunch Quiche
Coco-Fruit Salad
Sour Cream Lemon
Pound Cake**

Serves 6

For the last several years I have had a special Christmas luncheon for all my girlfriends whom I haven't seen enough during the year. We get together early enough in the day that those who need to pick up children at school can do so and still enjoy the party. I serve the Light Lunch Quiche and Coco-Fruit Salad buffet style and let each lady take as much or as little as she wants. This light luncheon has become the traditional Christmas brunch menu and is always very popular with the ladies.

Additionally, Chuck likes this meal for a light late-night supper. Since he is currently in school, he frequently doesn't get home until 8:00. Dinner waits until he arrives and by then we are both starving, but since we will be in bed soon we don't want a heavy, major meal. This light lunch menu is perfect for a late-night dinner. Chuck also likes this meal because all of it works well for leftovers. Even though the entire menu serves six, I frequently make it for the two of us. I take some to work for lunch and we have it the next night for dinner again.

Sunday brunch is another excellent choice for this collection of quiche, fresh fruit, and pound cake. Much of it can be prepared the night before. You can go to church, invite some friends over, and pop the quiche in the oven when you get home. With almost no effort you'll have a beautiful brunch and your guests will be wondering how you put it all together so quickly.

Timetable

The night before serving:

Make the pie crust if you don't already have one in the freezer.
Cut up all the fruit except the bananas.
Make and bake the pound cake, wrap tightly.

50 minutes before serving:

Prepare the quiche.

35 minutes before serving:

Cook the quiche.

10 minutes before serving:

Peel and cut the bananas, combine the fruit, arrange the fruit on individual plates, and top with flaked coconut.

Shopping List

Stock Items

___ Unbaked pie shell   ___ Bacon
___ Milk   ___ Eggs
___ Cornstarch   ___ Nutmeg
___ Salt   ___ Pepper
___ Butter   ___ Sugar
___ Flour   ___ Baking soda
___ Vanilla

Special Purchases

___ 1 small onion
___ Whipping cream
___ ¾ pound Swiss cheese
___ 3 bananas
___ 3 kiwifruit
___ Cantaloupe or honeydew melon
___ 3 grapefruit
___ 1 pint (basket) strawberries
___ 1 small package flaked coconut
___ 1 lemon
___ Sour cream

❦ *Light Lunch Quiche* ❦

Preheat oven to 400 degrees.

1 unbaked pie shell (See Marita's Pie Crust recipe,
     p. 174.)
4 slices bacon, cut into ¼-inch pieces
1 small onion, chopped
1 cup milk

½ cup whipping cream
3 tablespoons cornstarch
3 tablespoons milk
3 eggs
¼ teaspoon freshly grated nutmeg
½ teaspoon salt
¼ teaspoon pepper
¾ pound of Swiss cheese

In a medium saucepan, heat the 1 cup of milk and the whipping cream over medium-low heat. Meanwhile, in a cup or small bowl mix the 3 tablespoons of milk with the cornstarch until it forms a thick, pastelike, smooth mixture. Just before the milk boils, add the cornstarch/milk mixture and stir constantly until the mixture thickens and is almost as thick as yogurt, about 2 minutes. Remove the milk mixture from the heat and allow to cool.

In a small frying pan, cook the bacon over medium heat until it is limp. Add the chopped onion and continue cooking until the onion is soft, stirring occasionally. Meanwhile, in the food processor with the grater blade in place, grate the Swiss cheese. When the bacon and onion mixture is soft but not brown, remove it from the heat and set it aside.

In a medium bowl, beat the 3 eggs until they are light in color. Mix in the seasoning: nutmeg, salt, and pepper. Add the grated cheese and the cooled milk mixture. Stir to blend. Add the bacon and onion.

Pour the whole mixture into the crust and cook at 400 degrees for 35 minutes. When the quiche is fully cooked the top will have a nice golden brown glazed color and the whole pie will be full and puffy. It will settle down as it cools or is cut. Because it looks so pretty while it is still puffy, you might want to cut it at the table.

🐾 *Coco-Fruit Salad* 🐾

3 bananas
3 kiwifruit
1 cantaloupe or honeydew melon
3 grapefruit
1 basket strawberries or other berries in season
1 cup flaked coconut
1 lemon

Peel and slice the bananas and kiwifruit. Cut the melon into wedges and then cut off the rind. Cut the meat of the melon into bite-size pieces. Clean and hull the berries (if available). Combine all the fruit in a large bowl. Juice the lemon and pour the lemon juice over the fruit. Stir the fruit to coat with the lemon juice.

Peel and slice the grapefruit. Arrange several slices of grapefruit on each plate. Top with the fruit mixture and garnish with the flaked coconut.

All of the fruit can be cut up ahead, covered, and stored for as long as overnight except for the bananas. If the Coco-Fruit Salad is made in advance leave the banana out until just before serving.

❦ *Sour Cream Lemon Pound Cake* ❦

Preheat oven to 325 degrees

1 stick butter
1½ cups sugar
3 eggs, separated
1½ cups flour
⅛ teaspoon baking soda
½ teaspoon vanilla
½ cup sour cream
1 grated lemon rind, yellow part only

Generously coat a loaf pan with butter or other shortening.

In a cup or small bowl, slightly soften the stick of butter in the microwave, about 1 minute.

In a small bowl, using an electric mixer, beat the 3 egg whites until they are stiff.

In a medium bowl, using an electric mixer, beat the butter and sugar until they reach a creamy consistency. One at a time, add the egg yolks, beating after each addition. Sift the flour and the baking soda together onto a large piece of waxed paper or into a bowl. Add the flour mixture and the sour cream to the egg mixture as follows: Add approximately ½ cup of the flour mixture, then add a couple tablespoons of sour cream and stir with a spoon to blend. Repeat this process until all the flour and sour cream is used up. Add the vanilla and lemon rind and stir to blend.

Carefully fold the beaten egg whites into the batter. Pour the batter into the buttered loaf pan and bake for 1 hour and 15 minutes. When the cake is done the top will be lightly browned with a crack down the center and the cake will feel fairly firm when pressed.

Allow to cool for at least 5 minutes before serving. Sour Cream Lemon Pound Cake can be eaten warm but the flavors will be richer the next day. Slice like bread and serve with ice cream if desired.

Kids' Helps

Light Luncheon Quiche: Have the children help with this menu by pressing the cheese through the food processor. They can crack open the eggs, empty them into the bowl and beat them. While you add the seasoning, they can stir the mixture. With your help they can add the cheese, the cooled milk mixture, and the bacon and onion, stirring them all together.

Coco-Fruit Salad: Since it is unwise to allow young children to work with knives, the best way for kids to help with this is to stir the fruit and top the fruit with coconut.

Sour Cream Lemon Pound Cake: Once you have separated the eggs, a child can hold the beater and beat the egg whites. Then he or she can beat the butter and sugar and continue beating while you add the egg yolks. As you add the flour and sour cream a child can easily stir the batter to blend the ingredients.

Saturday Night Beanies and Weenies

Boston Baked Beans
Quick Brown Bread
Lemon Custard Cups

Serves 6

My mother's family grew up outside of Boston. My mother says every Saturday night they had baked beans for dinner. She grew up thinking that was the way everyone ate on Saturday night. When she had her own family she tried to serve baked beans with hot dogs. But my father grew up in the New York City area and he didn't care much for "beanies and weenies," so when I was growing up we frequently had my mother's traditional Saturday night dinner when my father was out of town.

I had forgotten about this meal until a recent trip to Boston, a trip that resulted from a romantic notion I'd had about going to New England to grandma's for Thanksgiving dinner. I'd pictured a Norman Rockwell scene in my mind and Chuck and I decided to go for it. But since my grandmother was no longer living, I called Aunt Jean to see if we could be invited to her home for Thanksgiving dinner.

We left home on Friday night and spent a few days in Boston before going to Aunt Jean's. We did the whole Freedom Trail walk and saw Paul Revere's house, Bunker Hill, and the Old North Church. While all of that history was great, one of the most memorable things we did was to have dinner at Durgin Park Restaurant, near Faneuil Hall. Everyone said we had to go there. They are famous for real Boston Baked Beans! Of course being there and eating beans brought back lots of memories for me and I told Chuck we had to buy a cookbook with a Boston Baked Beans recipe. On the way out I discovered their matchbook had their baked bean recipe inside. However, when I tried to make it, I realized the recipe was missing some key instructions. After several tries I have finally come up with a version that seems to work great and has a little less sugar than the original version.

Timetable

The night before serving:

Place beans in a large pot and cover with water. Be sure there are at least 2 inches of water over the top of the beans.

6 hours before serving or in the morning:

Drain the beans through a colander or strainer.
Rinse the beans and set aside.
Prepare onion.
Cut salt pork into bite-size cubes.
Combine beans, onion, and salt pork.
Cook in a 325-degree oven.

1 hour before serving:

Add hot dogs.
Prepare Quick Brown Bread.
Add brown bread to oven.
Prepare Lemon Custard Cups.

45 minutes before serving:

Add Lemon Custard Cups to the oven.

Shopping List

Stock Items

___ Sugar
___ Dry mustard
___ Ground pepper
___ Baking soda
___ Shortening
___ Vegetable oil
___ Eggs

___ Molasses
___ Salt
___ Whole wheat flour
___ Baking powder
___ Flour
___ Milk

Special Purchases

___ 1 pound small white beans
___ 1 small onion
___ 1 package hot dogs
___ Lemons to make ⅓ cup juice
___ ½–⅓ pound salt pork

❧ Boston Baked Beans ❧

1 pound small white beans
½–¾ pound salt pork

2 tablespoons sugar
⅓ cup molasses
1 teaspoon dry mustard
1 teaspoon salt
Several shakes of pepper
1 onion
5 cups water
5 hot dogs

The night before serving:

Place beans in a large ovenproof pot. Fill the pot with water, be sure to have at least 2 inches of water above the top of the beans. Let beans soak overnight.

6 hours before serving, or the morning before:

Drain the beans in a strainer or colander. Rinse in cold water. Set aside.

Peel the onion, cut off the stem and root, and place in the bottom of the large pot. Cut the salt pork into bite-size, 1-inch pieces. Place half of the salt pork in the bottom of the pan, around the onion. Add the beans to the pot. Place the remaining salt pork on the beans.

In a medium bowl combine the sugar, dry mustard, salt, and pepper. Add the molasses. Mix well. Add 1 cup of hot water. Mix well. Add remaining 4 cups of water. Stir. Pour mixture over the beans. Cover the pot and place in the oven at 325 degrees and cook for 6 hours.

In the last hour:

Add the hot dogs. Stir them in, recover, and continue to cook for the last hour.

Serve in bowls with hot brown bread on the side.

❧ *Quick Brown Bread* ❧

When I was a kid we had Boston Baked Beans out of the can and Boston Brown Bread, also out of a can. Real Boston Brown Bread is made in a can and steamed for several hours in the oven. Frankly I think that is too much work. I like this quick version.

Butter
1 egg
¼ cup solid shortening, such as Crisco
½ cup molasses
1 cup milk
2 cups whole wheat flour
1 teaspoon salt
½ teaspoon baking soda
1½ teaspoons baking powder
½ cup raisins

Generously butter a loaf pan.

In a small bowl, lightly beat the egg using an electric beater. Add the shortening and beat it until it is creamy. Add the molasses and milk, beating after each addition.

In a medium bowl, combine all the dry ingredients. Add the liquids and stir well. The mixture will be very thick. Pour into the prepared loaf pan and bake with the baked beans at 325 degrees for 1 hour.

Allow the bread to cool for 5 minutes before cutting.

🥢 *Lemon Custard Cups* 🥢

This casual, hearty dinner calls for a light dessert like these Lemon Custard Cups. Mix all the ingredients together and while they are cooking they separate into a rich custard on the bottom and a light cake on the top.

1 cup sugar
¼ cup flour
2 tablespoons vegetable oil
Dash of salt
2 teaspoons grated lemon peel
⅓ cup fresh lemon juice
1½ cups milk
3 eggs, separated

In a small pot, heat milk just to the point of boiling. Remove milk from the burner and set aside.

In a medium bowl, combine the sugar, flour, oil, and salt. Add lemon peel and lemon juice.

In a small bowl, beat the egg yolks. Stir in the milk. Add to the dry ingredients.

In a separate small bowl, beat the egg whites with an electric beater until they form stiff points when the beaters are lifted out. Be sure the beaters are completely clean before beating the egg whites. Fold the egg whites into the lemon mixture and pour into 6 ovenproof custard cups.

Bake at 325 degrees for 45 minutes or until the cake part is a light golden brown.

Custards can be served hot, room temperature, or chilled.

Kids' Helps

Boston Baked Beans: Once the onion is peeled let the kids put the onion in the bottom of the pot. They can place half of the cubed salt pork around the onion and place the remaining half on top of the beans once they have been added to the pot. Toward the end of the cooking time let the kids add the hot dogs.

Quick Brown Bread: Allow children to help with this recipe by cracking open the eggs and emptying them into the bowl. They can beat the eggs and continue beating after you add the other ingredients. They can also help by stirring the liquids into the dry ingredients.

Lemon Custard Cups: Kids can stir the sugar, flour, oil, and salt together and then stir in the lemon peel and juice. Once you have separated the eggs, let the children beat the yolks with the beater. After you add the milk, they can stir it in and then they can stir the liquids and dry ingredients to blend them. Allow them to beat the egg whites until they form stiff peaks. To help them learn cooking skills, be sure to point out what stiff peaks are and how to tell if the egg whites have reached that point.

New England Boiled Dinner

New England
Boiled Dinner
Aunt Jean's Beets
Tapioca Cream

Serves 8

With my New England roots this menu brings up fond memories for me. I suggest you serve this on Saint Patrick's Day for a proper Irish corned beef and cabbage dinner. It is also excellent for any cool winter night when you have time to allow it to simmer for the three or four hours needed. Its cooking will warm up the kitchen and give the whole house a warm, cozy fragrance.

When I got married I wanted to make this favorite dish of my childhood. It was something my grandmother always made and since she was no longer alive when I wanted the recipe, I called on her sister, my Aunt Jean. When Aunt Jean came to visit she brought me this recipe. While it does take a while to cook, it is very easy to make. Everything goes into one pot and boils until it is done. It is a favorite at my house and I am sure your family will love it as well.

Timetable

4 hours before serving:
Heat water.
Rinse corned beef.
Add spices and meat to boiling water.
Prepare Tapioca Cream.

1 hour before serving:
Peel and slice vegetables.

45 minutes before serving:
Add vegetables to boiling water.

20 minutes before serving:
Cut cabbage into eighths.
Bring a medium pot of water to a boil for the beets.

15 minutes before serving:
Add cabbage to boiling water.
Add beets to the separate pot of water.

Shopping List

Stock Items

___ Butter   ___ Eggs
___ Milk   ___ Sugar
___ Salt   ___ Vanilla

Special Purchases
___ 4 pounds corned-beef brisket

___ 6 medium carrots
___ 10 small red potatoes
___ 2 medium turnips
___ 1 head cabbage
___ 1 large onion
___ 8 small beets
___ quick-cooking tapioca

❧ *New England Boiled Dinner* ❧

4 pounds corned-beef brisket, flat cut
6 medium carrots
10 small red potatoes
2 medium turnips, about 2 inches in diameter
1 head cabbage
1 large onion
Butter

Bring a large pot of water to a boil over medium-high heat.

Remove corned beef from package and rinse. Add the spices and corned beef to the water. Corned beef usually comes in a package with the spices in a separate little packet. Continue to boil for about 3 hours (or 45 minutes per pound). If the water keeps boiling over, turn the temperature down to medium.

While the meat is cooking, peel the potatoes, carrots, and turnips. Cut the carrots into 2-inch pieces. If the top part of the carrot is especially thick, cut those pieces in half lengthwise so that their thickness is similar to the pieces from the thinner end. Cut the turnip into quarters. Peel the onion, leaving enough of the root section on to hold the onion together. Cut the onion into quarters. Forty-five minutes before serving add the vegetables to the corned beef. Continue to boil.

Cut the cabbage into quarters, starting at the root end and cutting straight through to the other side. Cut each piece in half lengthwise so that you now have 8 even wedge-shaped pieces. Fifteen minutes before serving, place the cabbage pieces on top of the vegetables and corned beef. Cover and continue to cook for 15 minutes.

To serve, remove cabbage and vegetables and arrange on a platter. Top with thin slices of butter. Remove corned beef and place on a cutting board. Cut into slices that are about ¼-inch thick and add the corned beef to the platter. Pass at the table with mustard for the corned beef.

🐾 *Aunt Jean's Beets* 🐾

Aunt Jean says this meal also needs some beets for color.

8 small beets, about 1 inch in diameter
Butter

Bring a medium pot of water to a boil. Add the beets and continue to boil for 15 minutes. Remove them from the heat and drain the water from the pot. Add cool water. One by one remove the beets and squeeze them. They will pop right out of their skins! Arrange them on the platter with the other vegetables and top with thin slices of butter. Do not boil the beets with the other vegetables. Their deep color will turn everything else red.

🏵 *Tapioca Cream* 🏵

When we used to go to my grandmother's house for New England Boiled Dinner, she always had Tapioca Cream for dessert.

2 eggs, separated
4 cups milk
⅓ cup quick-cooking tapioca
½ cup sugar
¼ teaspoon salt
1 teaspoon vanilla

In a medium saucepan, lightly beat the 2 egg yolks. Mix in 2 tablespoons of the milk. Add tapioca, sugar, salt, and remaining milk. Bring this mixture to a boil over medium heat, stirring constantly. Once it boils remove it from the heat. (Mixture will be thin.)

In a medium bowl, beat egg whites until they are stiff. When you remove the beaters the egg whites should form stiff little points that just barely fold over at the top.

Fold the hot mixture into the egg whites. Add the vanilla. Spoon into eight individual dessert dishes and chill for several hours. To serve, top with a cherry or strawberry for garnish.

Kids' Helps

New England Boiled Dinner: There isn't much for kids to do with this meal, but if they are old enough they could help by peeling the potatoes and carrots.

Tapioca Cream: Once you have separated the eggs, allow the kids to beat the egg yolk and then stir while you add the remaining ingredients. Using clean beaters, let them beat the egg whites.

American as Apple Pie

**Individual Meat Loaves
Scalloped Potatoes
Mixed Fresh Vegetables
Apple Pie**

Serves 6

This is Chuck's very favorite meal. Actually any meal that ends with a fresh homemade apple pie is his favorite but when the pie is combined with meat loaf and scalloped potatoes it becomes his *very* favorite. He puts up with the vegetables because he knows that he should eat them. If I have done something wrong, wrecked the car, forgotten to get the dry cleaning or ruined one of Chuck's shirts in the washing machine, I make him a fresh apple pie and all is forgiven. When I have been on the road too long the first thing I do on returning is to make an apple pie. It helps me feel like I am at home again, and when Chuck knows he will get an apple pie upon my return he is more eager to let me go.

In fact I don't know a man who wouldn't pick this meal over almost any other. They may pretend to enjoy all those little vegetables that are cut up to look like flowers and placed in a sauce that is too pretty to eat, but every man I know will always choose meat loaf and apple pie.

All of the ingredients in this menu are fresh and yet all of the recipes are easy to make. The entire menu can be prepared in about one hour.

Since this is a traditional and homey Americana meal you will want to set the table with your casual settings.

Timetable

Sometime earlier:

Prepare and freeze the pie crust.

1 hour before serving:

Prepare and cook Individual Meat Loaves.

50 minutes before serving:

Prepare and cook the Scalloped Potatoes.

40 minutes before serving:

Prepare and bake Crumb Top Apple Pie (in order to prepare the apple pie in the 15-minute time frame I suggest, you will need a clever little gadget that peels, cores, and slices the apples in one swift motion. For more information on this item please see Chapter 9, "Kitchen Basics").

10 minutes before serving:

Prepare and cook Fresh Mixed Vegetables.

Shopping List

Stock Items

—— Eggs
—— Salt
—— Marjoram
—— Pepper
—— Basil
—— Brown sugar
—— Flour
—— Olive oil

—— Butter
—— Thyme
—— Bay leaves
—— Parsley
—— Cinnamon
—— Sugar
—— Nuts
—— Butter Flavor Crisco

Special Purchases

—— 1½ pounds ground beef
—— 1 medium onion
—— 8 medium boiling potatoes
—— 3 medium zucchini squash
—— Cherry tomatoes
—— 6-8 green apples
—— Lemon
—— Chicken broth
—— Chili sauce
—— Stuffing mix

❦ *Individual Meat Loaves* ❦

Preheat oven to 350 degrees.

1½ pounds ground beef
2 eggs
1 cup prepared stuffing mix (I use Stove Top
San Francisco Style.)

1 8-ounce can of tomato sauce
1 medium onion, chopped
1½ teaspoons salt
¼ teaspoon thyme
¼ teaspoon marjoram

½ cup chili sauce
6 small bay leaves

In a large bowl, mix all the ingredients except the chili sauce and bay leaves. (The best way to mix this is to roll up your sleeves and squeeze the mixture through your hands. Your hands will get covered with the mixture anyway when you shape the loaves.)

On a cookie sheet or shallow baking pan, shape the meat mixture into 6 little oval-shaped loaves. Top each loaf with 1–2 tablespoons chili sauce and lay a bay leaf on the chili sauce.

Bake in the preheated 350-degree oven 45–60 minutes or until richly browned.

🐾 *Scalloped Potatoes* 🐾

Preheat oven to 350 degrees.

8 medium boiling potatoes (the smallish white potatoes)
1 teaspoon salt
¼ teaspoon pepper

½ teaspoon parsley
1¼ cups grated Swiss or cheddar cheese
6 tablespoons butter (¾ stick)
1 cup chicken broth

Generously butter an oval or rectangular baking dish, approximately 9 x 12 x 2 inches.

If you prefer your potatoes without skin, peel the potatoes. Using the food processor, slice the potatoes.

Arrange half of the potatoes in the bottom of the baking pan. Sprinkle them with half of the salt, pepper, parsley, and cheese. Cut the butter into thin slices and place half of them on top of the potato layer. Repeat the entire process for the next layer, starting with the potatoes and finishing with the butter. Pour the chicken broth over the top. Bake until the potatoes are tender and the top has a golden brown crust, about 45 minutes. Serve immediately.

❦ *Mixed Fresh Vegetables* ❦

If you have a vegetable garden or know someone who does, you know there are several vegetables that produce more vegetables on a few plants than you can eat yourself. Two of them are squash and cherry tomatoes. This recipe is an excellent way to utilize that abundance. Also, since these are abundant vegetables, they are usually an economical purchase which adds to the Americana nature of this entire menu.

3 medium zucchini squash
3 small yellow squash
⅓ cup olive oil
1 cup cherry tomatoes
4 teaspoons minced fresh basil or 1 teaspoon
    of dried basil
Salt
Freshly ground pepper

Trim the squashes and cut into ¾-inch slices. Using a microwave steamer, steam the squashes for about 3 minutes, until they are just crisp-tender. (To steam vegetables in the microwave, place a couple of table-spoons of water in the bottom of the steamer. Put the vegetables in the top portion and cover.)

Using a large frying pan, heat the oil over medium-high heat. Add the squash and stir lightly to coat them with the oil. Add the tomatoes and basil. Continue to stir lightly for about 1 minute or until the vegetables get slightly browned. Sprinkle with salt and pepper and serve.

❦ *Crumb Top Apple Pie* ❦

This pie is so easy to make I wonder why anyone buys a frozen pie. It is a bit different from most apple pies in that it has very little sugar and therefore it doesn't have that gooey jelly-like texture. All you taste is the apples and seasoning. When I prepared this pie on TBN's "Joy" program, I got more requests for this recipe than any I have ever done.

If you are in a real time crunch you can use a frozen store-bought crust but you will not have the entire great product that you will have with this perfect pie crust. Since the recipe makes enough crust for two single-crust pies, you can easily make up two crusts and keep one of them in the freezer for future use. An even better idea is to make up several crusts at a time and keep them in the freezer.

The crust recipe is very easy. I have included complete instructions for making it so that the novice pie maker will know exactly what to do. Don't let making pie crust intimidate you. A good pie crust is well worth the little extra effort it takes.

Preheat the oven to 400 degrees.

1 unbaked pie crust
6-8 green apples, peeled, cored, and sliced (I use Granny Smith apples.)
2 tablespoons sugar
½ teaspoon cinnamon
Juice of ½ lemon

½ cup brown sugar
½ cup flour
½ stick butter
Handful of nuts, your choice (I use pecans.)

In a large bowl (can be the same bowl as the one used for the crust—don't bother to wash it but be sure to dump any crust remnants out) combine the apples, sugar, cinnamon, and lemon juice. I mix it with my hands. Pour this mixture into the unbaked pie crust.

In the same bowl, combine the brown sugar, flour, butter, and nuts. Using a pastry blender, slice the butter and mix until the mixture has a crumbly consistency. Sprinkle the topping over the apples. If you are using a lot of apples or very large apples the pie will be very high and some of the topping usually rolls off. I place the pie on a cookie sheet before adding the topping; then when it rolls off I collect it up carefully and put it back on the pie.

Bake the pie for about 45 minutes or until it is nicely browned. Keep an eye on it. Sometimes you may need to place a piece of foil on the top of the crumbly topping to keep the peak from getting too dark.

Let the pie cool for about 10 minutes before serving. I think it is best with a big scoop of vanilla ice cream dripping over each piece, but you can serve it any way you like.

If you are preparing the pie and the meat loaf at the same time as I have suggested, cook it at the same temperature as the meat loaf until you remove the meat loaf from the oven. Then raise the temperature to 400 degrees. Cooking the pie at this lower temperature will take a little more cooking time.

❦ *Marita's Pie Crust* ❦

Makes 2 single-crust pies

2 cups regular flour (I use unbleached although any
    regular flour will work fine.)
1 teaspoon salt

¾ cup Butter Flavor Crisco (use only Butter Flavor
    Crisco, very important)
¼ cup water

In a large bowl, combine the flour and salt. Using a pastry blender mix in the Butter Flavor Crisco until the particles are pea-sized and the mixture looks like coarse cornmeal. Sprinkle the mixture with the water and toss with a fork to combine. Using your hands, reach into the bowl and press the mixture into a ball.

Don't worry if there are little bits that don't mix in. Be careful to handle the dough as little as possible. It is not like bread dough where you need to knead it frequently—overhandling makes pie crust tough.

Use a pastry cloth on the counter and a pastry sleeve on the rolling pin. These are important items for a perfect crust. Sprinkle flour on the pastry cloth and roll the rolling pin in the flour to coat the pastry sleeve.

Once the dough is in a ball, break the ball in half and shape into another ball. On the pastry cloth, press the ball down until it looks like a thick pancake. Roll the dough with strokes from the center out using the rolling pin. Once the dough is at least 1 inch larger than the edge of the pie plate, stop rolling. Place the pie plate on top of the dough, face down. Cut the edge of the dough about 2 fingers width from the edge of the pie plate. Remove the edge pieces. Leave the pie plate on the dough and fold the edges of the pastry cloth over the pie plate. With your hand, reach under the pastry cloth so your hand is in the center of the crust and flip the whole thing over. Peel off the pastry cloth.

Your crust should now be perfectly centered on the pie plate. If it is not, adjust it. Fold under the edges that are hanging over the rim of the pie plate; crimp them to make a pretty edge. To crimp, lightly pinch the edge with both hands. With one thumb and forefinger press the dough inward and with the other thumb and forefinger press out. Continue this technique all around the crust.

Repeat the previous steps for the second crust.

If you are only using one crust, wrap the other tightly in plastic wrap or place in a large zippered storage bag and freeze. The crust will last nicely for several weeks. To bake an empty pie crust, prick it all over with a fork and bake it in a 425-degree oven 10-15 minutes, until golden brown. (Do not bake the crust first if you are using it for the apple pie.)

Kids' Helps

Individual Meat Loaves: Kids can unwrap the ground beef and place it in a large bowl. They can crack open the eggs and empty them into the bowl and open the stuffing mix package and add it to the bowl. Once you have opened the can of tomato sauce and chopped the onion they can add those ingredients. You will want to measure the seasonings, but you can let a child add them. Once all the ingredients are in the bowl, let the kids reach into the bowl and squeeze and squish the ingredients until they are blended.

Scalloped Potatoes: Let the children press the potatoes through the food processor to slice them. They can arrange half of the sliced potatoes in the bottom of the baking dish and help sprinkle the seasonings and cheese on top of the potatoes.

Mixed Fresh Vegetables: Once all the vegetables are cut and the zucchini are steamed, let the children help by stirring the vegetables while they cook.

Crumb Top Apple Pie (crust): Other than adding the premeasured ingredients to the bowl, there isn't much that little ones can do to help with this process. Once the crust is made, you can show them how to crimp the edges of the crust and let them give it a try.

Crumb Top Apple Pie: If you are using the apple peeler-corer-slicer, let the kids turn the crank. They will think it's great fun to watch the peelings come off in skinny little strips. Once you have cut the apple slices in half, let the children put the slices into a bowl. They can mix all the ingredients with their hands. For the topping, children can add the ingredients to the bowl if you help them measure them out.

Australian Dinner

Pumpkin Soup
Honey Roast Lamb
Roast Potatoes
Scalloped Tomatoes
Damper Bread
Pavlova

When I went to Australia several years ago I looked for foods that were "Australian." We dined in several private homes and in numerous restaurants and I learned a lot about Australia. I learned that Australia is a very young country. Discovered only 200 years ago, Australia is even younger than the United States. It was started as a penal colony that England used to relieve the overcrowding in its prisons. So while Australia has its roots in England, the original settlers were probably not terribly interested in culture or fine cooking.

Additionally, like America, Australia is a melting pot of people. Because of the diverse background of its people you are just as likely to find food influenced by China, Japan, and India on a menu as you are to find food with English roots. As a result it is difficult to truly define "Australian cooking."

In my search, however, I did come up with several

items that seemed to be universally present in almost every Australian restaurant we visited. Plan a special night to learn about Australia. Get out the globe and show the family where it is. Maybe even check a picture book out of the library and learn about the beautiful landscape before enjoying its wonderful food. You could even practice speaking "Australian."

Yes, the Australians speak English, but it is a different English than we speak in America and if you don't pay close attention you may totally miss what they are saying. Here are a few of the most adoptable expressions. Australians say "g'day" for hello or good-bye. Rather than saying "you're welcome" when someone says "thank you," Aussies say "no worry" meaning it was no problem. If someone is going to do something right away they do it "straight away," and of course a good friend is a "mate." As you sit down at the table you might greet each other by saying "g'day." When someone thanks you for passing the butter, say "no worry," and if you are asked to do the dishes, say you'll get to it "straight away."

Timetable

4 hours before serving:

Prepare Pavlova meringue.

2½ hours before serving:

Prepare leg of lamb, place in the covered dish, and cook.

2 *hours before serving:*
Prepare Damper.

1³⁄₄ *hours before serving:*
Place Damper in the oven.

1¹⁄₄ *hours before serving:*
Peel pumpkin and potatoes.
Slice onion.

1 *hour before serving:*
Remove the Damper from the oven.
Cook onion in the saucepan.
Add the pumpkin, broth, and salt and bring to a boil.
Prepare the Scalloped Tomatoes.
Boil the potatoes.

45 *minutes before serving:*
Remove the leg of lamb from the covered pot and
   place in roasting pan.
Add potatoes to the roast.
Boil the pan drippings down to a glaze and pour over
   the roast.

30 *minutes before serving:*
Place the roast and potatoes in the oven.
Place Scalloped Tomatoes in the oven.

10 *minutes before serving:*
Puree the pumpkin and return it to the saucepan.
Add the remaining ingredients.
Keep soup warm over low heat.

To serve:

Remove roast from the oven.

Slice the roast.

Prepare plates by placing sliced roast, potatoes, and
Scalloped Tomatoes attractively on the plates.
Top the roast and the potatoes with pan juices.

Shopping List

Stock Items

___ Butter

___ Pepper

___ Ginger

___ Honey

___ Self-rising flour

___ Eggs

___ Cornstarch

___ Salt

___ Nutmeg

___ Rosemary

___ Sugar

___ Milk

___ White vinegar

___ Vanilla

Special Purchases

___ 2 onions (1 small, 1 medium)

___ Fresh pumpkin

___ 3 cans chicken broth

___ Whipping cream

___ Sour cream

___ Chives

___ 3–4 pound leg of lamb

___ Apple cider

___ 10 small red potatoes

___ 3–4 tomatoes

___ Bread crumbs

___ 5 bananas

___ 1 pint (basket) strawberries

___ ½ pint (small basket) raspberries

🦌 *Pumpkin Soup* 🦌

The first item is a real surprise to all my American friends and my Australian friends are amused that this dish is not common to Americans. The most frequently offered item I found in restaurants throughout Australia was pumpkin soup. Yes, pumpkin soup. I know it doesn't sound very exotic and may not strike you as something that is Australian but it is a very traditional entree there. It surprises us Americans because we think of pumpkin as a dessert item. We of course have pumpkin pie, pumpkin muffins, and pumpkin cookies. But really pumpkin is a vegetable, a member of the squash family, and soup is a more logical use for squash than pie or cookies.

Throughout Australia I tried several different styles of pumpkin soup. Some had chunks of pumpkin boiled in a broth base, others were a pumpkin base mixed with other vegetables, but I liked the creamy pureed style that I have included here the best. Once Halloween is over, cook up your decorations. It is a very economical thing to do with your pumpkins when you are done using them to make your home festive.

1½ tablespoons butter
1 medium onion, peeled and sliced
2 pounds peeled pumpkin, cut into 1-inch cubes
6 cups chicken broth
½ teaspoon salt
Pinch of freshly grated nutmeg
4 tablespoons whipping cream
Freshly grated pepper

Sour cream
Chopped chives

In a large saucepan, melt the butter. Add the sliced onion and cook over low heat, stirring frequently until the onions are soft and glossy, approximately 10 minutes. Add the peeled and chopped pumpkin, the broth, and the salt. Bring the mixture to a boil over medium-high heat. Once it boils, turn the heat back down to low, cover that pan, and simmer for 45 minutes or until the pumpkin is very tender. Using a strainer and a large bowl, strain the liquid into the large bowl and set aside. In the food processor or blender, puree the pumpkin and onion until they are smooth and return the pureed mixture to the pan. Add the reserved liquid and stir to blend. Add the nutmeg and the cream. Lightly dust the top of the soup with the freshly ground pepper. Stir to blend. Taste the soup and add more cream, salt, or pepper if needed.

To serve the Pumpkin Soup, ladle it into bowls and top with about a tablespoon of sour cream. Sprinkle the sour cream with the chopped chives.

❦ *Honey Roast Lamb* ❦

Next is the main course. Try this delicious roast leg of lamb. Many Americans, including my husband, think that they don't like lamb. I think this is usually because they weren't served lamb growing up and therefore perceive lamb as a strange meat. My bet is that if you don't tell your family and friends what you are serving, the wonderful aroma that fills the house while the leg of lamb is cooking will tempt them to try it. Once they try it they will be sold. Be sure to use fresh American lamb. Its flavor is much milder than the frozen spring lamb we usually get from New Zealand.

1 leg of lamb, 3-4 pounds
Salt and freshly ground pepper
1½ teaspoons ground ginger

2-3 cups apple cider
1-2 inches fresh rosemary or 2 teaspoons dried
2 tablespoons honey

Rub the outside of the leg of lamb with the salt and pepper and the ginger. Place the lamb in a large, covered, flameproof casserole dish or a heavy, large saucepan with a lid. Pour the apple cider around the lamb. Add the honey and the rosemary. Cover. Simmer over low heat 2–2½ hours depending on the size of the lamb. Toward the end of the cooking time, check the lamb to be sure that it is not sticking on the bottom of the pan.

After simmering remove the lamb, place it in a roasting pan, and cover it with foil.

Using a small ladle, gently remove as much of the excess fat from the pan juices as possible. Boil the juices down to a glaze over medium-high heat. Pan juices can be left in the casserole or large pot for this step.

Spoon the glaze over the lamb and roast uncovered in a 350-degree oven for 30 minutes. This gives the lamb a beautiful honey glaze. If you are making the roast potatoes, they should be added before the leg of lamb goes into the oven.

❦ *Roast Potatoes* ❦

10 small red potatoes

Peel the potatoes and cut into quarters. In a medium pot of boiling water, boil the potatoes 5 minutes. Drain the water and add the quartered potatoes to the leg of lamb during the 30 minutes of roasting time.

❦ *Scalloped Tomatoes* ❦

One of the things that surprised me during my trip to Australia was the frequent use of tomatoes. While in America we use them primarily in salad, they become a cooked vegetable in Australia. They are even served with breakfast!

This recipe for Scalloped Tomatoes is an old-fashioned tradition with roast lamb. It also adds a nice spot of color to the plate. I love this recipe because it requires no measuring.

3 or 4 tomatoes
Salt
Pepper
Sugar

1 small onion, grated
Bread crumbs (can be purchased or you can make
   your own by chopping up white bread in the food
   processor)
Thyme
Butter

Grease a pie plate with butter. Place a layer of sliced tomatoes on the bottom of the pie plate. There will be some overlap of the tomatoes. Sprinkle with salt, pepper, and a tiny pinch of sugar. Cover with a thin layer of grated onion, then add a layer of bread crumbs. Sprinkle with thyme and dot with little pieces of butter. Repeat the layers until the pie plate is full, usually 2 or 3 layers. The top layer should be bread crumbs, thyme, and butter.

Cook in a 350-degree oven for 30 minutes. If the tomatoes are being cooked at the same time as the leg of lamb, add them to the oven at the same time as the lamb is put in to roast.

Cut and serve like pie.

🐾 *Damper or Bush Bread* 🐾

On my first trip to Australia I went to a little tourist song-and-dance show. In that show they told us about the history of Australia and served us Damper. They told us that Damper or Bush Bread was made by the cowboys when they were out in the bush. It is extremely simple to make and was customarily made in the coals of the campfire. This version is made in your regular oven so you don't have to go out to the "bush" to make it. It is so simple that you will wonder why you didn't know about it before—and you will probably want to make it for more than just this Australian menu.

Preheat oven to 400 degrees.

4 cups self-rising flour (*must* be self-rising)
2 teaspoons salt
1 tablespoon sugar
¾ cup milk
¾ cup water

1 egg, beaten with 2 tablespoons milk

Sift the flour and salt into a large bowl. Mix in the sugar. Make a well in the center of the dry ingredients in the bowl. Pour in the milk and water. Using two knives, blend quickly. Do not knead or mix with your hands. Once mixed simply empty it onto a lightly greased cookie sheet. Using a rubber spatula, roughly shape the dough into a round loaf. Brush the loaf with the beaten egg and milk before cooking. Bake for about 45 minutes or until the loaf is a nice golden color.

Slice into thick slices and serve with butter.

❦ *Pavlova* ❦

In my search for truly Australian food, everyone I talked with told me I had to have Pavlova. In fact I was told that it is the unofficial dessert of Australia. It is really very simple to make and it looks exotic. In reality it is just a meringue shell with assorted fruit and whipped cream. The trick comes in having the meringue crisp on the outside and marshmallowy inside.

Preheat oven to 400 degrees.

6 egg whites
Pinch of salt
1½ cups sugar
1½ teaspoons white vinegar
1½ teaspoons cornstarch
1 teaspoon of vanilla
2 cups whipping cream, whipped
5 bananas
1 pint strawberries
½ pint raspberries (or any additional
    fruit)

Using an ovenproof serving plate, grease the plate with butter and dust with cornstarch. Hold the plate upside down and tap on the bottom to remove excess cornstarch. Set aside.

Using an electric mixer, beat the egg whites and salt until they are stiff and form stiff points when the beaters are removed. Continue beating and add the sugar 1 tablespoon at a time until all the sugar is mixed into the egg whites. The meringue will be thick and shiny. Stir in the vinegar, the cornstarch, and the vanilla.

Pour the meringue onto the prepared serving plate. Spread almost to the edges of the plate being careful not to spread it too thin. The meringue should be at least 2½ inches high. Using a spatula create little peaks and valleys in the meringue and leave a slight indentation in the center.

Lower the oven temperature to 225 degrees and place the plate of meringue into the preheated oven. Cook for 1 hour and 45 minutes. Remove from the oven and allow to cool.

Just before serving fill the dip in the center with whipped cream and top with the sliced fresh fruit. Add a small dollop of whipped cream on the top for decoration. Slice and serve like pie.

Kids' Helps

Pumpkin Soup: Children can help out by stirring the onion as it cooks. Once all the ingredients have been cooked together, they can help with pureeing them by turning the food processor off and on. Once the soup is back in the pan they can stir the soup as you add the remaining liquid, the nutmeg, and the cream.

Honey Roast Lamb: Most children like to get their hands into things and rubbing the spices into the leg of lamb will be fun for them to do.

Roast Potatoes: If your children are old enough, they can peel the potatoes.

Scalloped Tomatoes: If you are making your own bread crumbs, let the children help by turning the food processor on and off until the bread has turned into crumbs. Once the tomatoes are sliced, let the children place them in the pie plate and sprinkle them with seasonings, grated onion, and bread crumbs.

Damper or Bush Bread: Once you have measured out the flour and salt, let the children sift it and then stir in the sugar. They can pour in the milk and water if you have it premeasured, but you should do the mixing unless your children are older and more advanced in their cooking skills. After you have mixed the dough and shaped it, let the children brush the loaf with the egg and milk mixture.

Pavlova: Have the children help you with the pavlova by beating the egg whites until they form stiff peaks. Have them continue beating while you add the sugar.

❦ English Pub Meal ❦

Toad in the Hole
Steamed Broccoli with Lemon Butter
Strawberry-Blueberry Fool

Serves 6

For our second anniversary Chuck and I went to England. We spent a few days in London and then we headed out to the country. We stayed in several charming country inns. One of them was built in the fourteenth century and had stone walls that had to be at least 12 inches thick. The other was a lovely manor house out in the middle of nowhere. There wasn't another building in sight. It was a large gray stone building with a long, tree-lined drive heading up to the arched entryway. In these romantic spots we fell in love with English food.

While English food has long been disparaged by gourmets because of its bland flavors, we appreciated its simplicity. It isn't full of things you can't pronounce or odd-looking items you are afraid to eat. It is basic, practical, and real.

This pub menu features a standard pub meal that has been updated just a bit to fit our American tastes. Since this is an everyday, rustic, homey type of meal, you will want to set the table with your more casual placemats and napkins and use the everyday stoneware.

If you have children this will be a wonderful time to get out the globe and show them the location of England. Eating foods from foreign lands will not only broaden their culinary horizons but will also give them an interest in learning geography. You might also want to check out a picture book on England from the library so that you can all see pictures of the English countryside, the popular pubs, and the English way of life, which is much simpler and slower than the fast-lane lives that most of us in America live.

Timetable

1½ hours before serving:

Prepare and chill the Strawberry-Blueberry Fool.
Preheat the oven to 425 degrees.

1 hour before serving:

Place the sausages in the oven.
Prepare the batter.

40 minutes before serving:

Remove the sausages from the oven.
Reduce the oven temperature to 400 degrees.
Cover the sausages with the batter and replace
  in the oven.

20 minutes before serving:
Prepare the broccoli.

10 minutes before serving:
Cook the broccoli.

Shopping List

Stock Items

___ Bacon drippings or
    vegetable oil
___ Pepper
___ Eggs
___ Butter
___ Vanilla

___ Flour
___ Salt
___ Milk
___ Freshly grated
    nutmeg
___ Sugar

Special Purchases

___ ½ pound skinless link sausages
___ Sharp cheddar cheese
___ Fresh parsley
___ 1–1½ pounds fresh broccoli
___ ½ lemon
___ 1 pint strawberries
___ 1 pint blueberries
___ 1 pint whipping cream

❦ Toad in the Hole ❦

I don't know where the name for this unusual dish
came from, but it is sure to arouse people's interest.
It was originally a way to use the leftover meat from

the Sunday roast and you could still use it that way if you choose. However, most people today make Toad in the Hole with sausages.

This recipe uses a batter like a Yorkshire pudding or popover. The meat is heated in a pie plate and the batter is poured over it. I am always amazed that when the Toad in the Hole is cooked, the heavy sausages float to the top. When it comes out of the oven the pastry has puffed up and risen 1-2 inches above the edge of the pie plate—and there raised in the top are the little sausages.

Preheat oven to 425 degrees.

1 tablespoon bacon drippings or vegetable oil
½ pound skinless link sausages
¾ cup flour
¼ teaspoon salt
¼ teaspoon pepper
¼ cup sharp cheddar cheese, grated
1¼ cup milk
2 eggs
½ teaspoon freshly grated nutmeg
2 tablespoons freshly snipped parsley

Using a glass pie plate, melt the bacon drippings or add the vegetable oil. Place the sausages in the pie plate with the drippings or oil and bake in the preheated 425-degree oven 15-20 minutes or until they are lightly browned. Turn the sausages several times during cooking to prevent sticking.

While the sausages cook, sift the flour, salt, and pepper into a medium bowl. Stir in the cheese. Using a small bowl and a hand-held whisk, beat the milk, egg, nutmeg, and parsley until they are well blended. Add a small amount of the milk mixture, approximately ¼ cup, to the flour mixture to make a smooth, stiff batter. Set the batter aside for 5 minutes.

Meanwhile, remove the sausages from the oven and reduce oven temperature to 400 degrees.

Once the batter has set for 5 minutes stir in the remaining milk mixture until it is well blended. Pour the batter into the pie plate over the sausages. Place it in the 400-degree oven and bake for 30 minutes or until the batter is light and puffy with a golden brown color.

To serve cut into 4 or 6 pieces and serve like pie.

❦ *Steamed Broccoli with Lemon Butter* ❦

When I had Toad in the Hole in an English pub it was served with fresh broccoli. Since broccoli is nearly always available and is inexpensive it works well with this economical meal. I suggest that it be cooked in a microwave steamer. This way it keeps its nice green color and retains its nutritional value.

1–1½ pounds fresh broccoli
1 tablespoon butter
Juice of ½ lemon

Trim the broccoli so that the heavy base stem is removed and the remaining pieces look like nice little trees that are about 2 inches long. If some of the "little trees" have a stem that is much thicker than the rest, cut the stem and branches in half lengthwise. Place the broccoli in the top half of the microwave vegetable steamer.

Place about 2 tablespoons of water in the bottom half of the steamer. Place the top half of the vegetable steamer with the broccoli over the bottom half and cover with the lid. Microwave 6–8 minutes.

Once the broccoli is cooked to your liking, remove it from the microwave, drain the water from the bottom, and transfer the broccoli to the bottom piece. Add the butter and the lemon juice. Replace the lid and shake to coat all the broccoli with the butter and lemon juice. Serve.

🍃 *Strawberry-Blueberry Fool* 🍃

1 pint strawberries
1 pint blueberries
1 cup milk
1 egg
1 egg yolk
3 teaspoons sugar
¼ teaspoon vanilla
1 cup whipping cream

Rinse the strawberries and blueberries and allow to drain. Remove the stems from the strawberries. Set 6 nice strawberries aside to use as garnish.

Using the food processor, puree the strawberries and blueberries. Set aside.

Make a pouring custard by heating the milk in a small saucepan over medium heat until it almost boils. Remove the milk from the heat. In a medium bowl, combine the egg, egg yolk, and sugar and stir until they are well blended. Stir in the cooled milk. Using a medium saucepan, bring about ½ cup of water to a boil over medium-high heat. Place the bowl with the egg and milk mixture on the pan so that the bottom of the bowl doesn't touch the water. Reduce the heat to medium-low and cook the custard in the bowl over the boiling water 10–15 minutes, stirring all the time with a wooden spoon, until the mixture thickens to that of heavy cream. Do not allow the custard to boil. Once the custard has thickened, remove the bowl from the heat and fold the fruit puree into the custard.

Using an electric beater, whip the cream in a small bowl until it is thick and stiff. Fold the whipped cream into the fruit/custard mixture. Spoon the mixture into dessert dishes and chill for 1 hour. Before serving top each dish with a fresh strawberry.

Kids' Helps

Toad in the Hole: Let the children sift the flour, salt, and pepper into a bowl. Then let them stir in the cheese.

Steamed Broccoli with Lemon Butter: Once the broccoli is cooked, let the children add the butter and lemon juice. They can shake the steamer to coat the broccoli with the lemon juice and butter.

Strawberry-Blueberry Fool: Once you have cleaned the berries, children can puree them by turning the food processor on and off. For the custard part, they can stir the egg mixture in the bowl over the boiling water. Kids can whip the cream, although you will want to help them hold the beater straight so the cream doesn't splatter all over the kitchen. They can fold the whipped cream into the fruit/custard mixture.

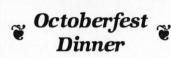

❧ *Octoberfest* ❧ *Dinner*

Bockwurst
Sauerkraut
Potato Pancakes
Apple-Topped
German Cake

Serves 6

This traditional and simple German meal is a favorite at my house. Both my husband and I are half German and although neither of us remembers eating a meal like this from our childhood I do know that this style of German apple cake is one of my father's favorites from *his* childhood. I remember eating meals like this on a trip to Germany. It is different but not strange, and its best feature is that it only takes 15 minutes to prepare.

This German meal is suitable for a company dinner. Set the table with placemats and napkins that are of a coarser fabric and use heavier stoneware and silverware. For a beverage offer apple juice.

This meal provides the atmosphere for a fun and casual evening. Don't think you need to wait until October to have it—it also makes an excellent summer barbecue.

Timetable

The evening or morning before serving:

Prepare and bake the Apple-Topped German Cake.

15 minutes before serving:

Prepare Potato Pancakes.
Place sauerkraut in a microwaveable serving dish.
Heat frying pan or griddle.
Turn on barbecue or broiler.

10 minutes before serving:

Cook Potato Pancakes.
Place Bockwurst on the barbecue or under the broiler.
Heat sauerkraut in the microwave oven.

5 minutes before serving:

Turn the Potato Pancakes.
Turn the Bockwurst.

To Serve:

Place 1 or 2 Bockwurst per person on the plate, add the sauerkraut and the Potato Pancake on the side.
Pass the mustard and sour cream separately.

Shopping List

Stock Items

___ Butter
___ Eggs

___ Sugar
___ Flour

___ Baking powder   ___ Vanilla
___ Cinnamon   ___ Salt
___ Pepper   ___ Prepared mustard

Special Purchases

___ 3 large green apples
___ Whipping cream
___ 3 medium potatoes
___ 1 onion
___ Sour cream
___ Sauerkraut, from a German market or deli
___ 6–8 Bockwurst or other German sausages,
    found in a German market or deli

❦ Apple-Topped German Cake ❦

Preheat oven to 350 degrees.

1 stick butter, melted
1 cup sugar
2 eggs
1 cup flour
1 teaspoon baking powder
1 teaspoon vanilla

½ cup sugar
1½ teaspoons cinnamon
3 large Granny Smith or Pippin apples

Coat an 8 x 8 inch square cake pan with shortening.

Using a large bowl and an electric mixer, combine the melted butter with the sugar and eggs and beat them until they are thoroughly blended.

Add the flour, baking powder, and vanilla and beat them until all the ingredients are well blended.

Pour the mixture into the prepared baking dish. Set aside.

Peel, core, and slice the apples into half-moon shapes. Place the apples in the large bowl. Sprinkle with the sugar and cinnamon. Using your hands or 2 large spoons, mix the apples to coat them with the cinnamon and sugar. Arrange the apples on top of the batter in overlapping rows. Press them lightly into the batter.

Bake in the preheated 350-degree oven for 1 hour. Cool. Serve at room temperature. Cut the cake into squares. Top with the whipped cream when serving.

🐾 *Whipped Cream* 🐾

1 cup whipping cream
1 tablespoon sugar
½ teaspoon vanilla

Pour the whipping cream into a small mixing bowl. Using the electric mixer, beat on high until soft peaks form. Add the sugar and vanilla and beat until blended.

❧ *Potato Pancakes* ❧

3 medium potatoes
1 medium onion
1 tablespoon salt
Dash of freshly ground pepper
1 lightly beaten egg
1½ cups flour
1 tablespoon butter, bacon fat, or lard
Sour cream

Using the food processor, grate the potatoes and the onion. Place the grated potato and onion in a medium bowl. Add the flour, salt, pepper, and egg and stir to blend.

Heat the skillet or griddle to medium-high and melt the shortening. Drop the pancake batter onto the heated surface in pancake-size portions and cook about 5 minutes on each side or until crisp and golden. When serving, pass the sour cream separately.

To prepare the rest of this meal, cook the Bockwurst, or other German sausage, on the barbecue or under the broiler for approximately 5 minutes per side. Serve with mustard.

Cook the sauerkraut in a microwaveable dish for 6–8 minutes.

Kids' Helps

Apple-Topped German Cake: Children can help out with this recipe by beating the butter, sugar, and eggs until they are blended. After you add the flour, baking powder, and vanilla, they can again beat them until they are all blended. If you have an apple peeler-corer-slicer, let the children turn the crank to peel and slice the apples. Then let them combine the apples and the spices with their hands.

Potato Pancakes: Children can press the potato and onion through the food processor to grate them. Then they can stir the potatoes and onions with the flour, salt, pepper, and egg. Let them drop the pancake batter by spoonfuls onto the griddle or skillet.

Spaghetti
Garlic Bread
Tomato, Onion and
Cucumber Salad
Almond Cream

Serves 6

Every now and then I get a craving for spaghetti but because Chuck doesn't like it I usually satisfy my craving in a restaurant. I am almost always disappointed. I have in mind a thick, rich sauce that is loaded with tomato chunks and full of meat, a sauce that has been simmering for several hours and fills the air with the inviting aroma of onion and garlic. The sauce I usually find in most restaurants is thin and canned-tasting.

Once in a while I just have to have the real thing, spaghetti like my mother used to make. I usually make it on a Sunday afternoon when there is plenty of time for the sauce to simmer. Even if this isn't the way your mother made her spaghetti, I am sure that you will want to adopt this as your family's recipe. My guests always tell me this is the best spaghetti sauce they have ever had and Chuck likes it better than most.

While the Spaghetti Sauce takes several hours to simmer to perfection, it is quick to prepare and the rest of the menu—the Garlic Bread; the Tomato, Onion, and Cucumber Salad; and the Almond Cream dessert are all quite simple. Together they make a perfect Sunday supper.

Since this recipe makes a large pot of sauce, why not invite some friends over for a fun and casual evening? Or save the leftover sauce. It reheats wonderfully for a lunch or dinner later in the week. In fact the sauce is even better the next day!

Set the table with your casual tableware. If you have a red-and-white-checked tablecloth, this is the time to use it. If you don't have one, use any other casual tablecloth and napkins. Serve the spaghetti and garlic bread on the everyday dishes with the salad in a bowl on the side. Turn the lights down and light the candles.

Timetable

3½ hours before serving:

Prepare the Spaghetti Sauce.

2½–3 hours before serving:

Prepare the Almond Cream.
Prepare the Tomato, Onion, and Cucumber Salad.
  (First prepare the first part of the Almond Cream and set it in the refrigerator. Then prepare the salad. By the time you have finished with the salad, the Almond Cream will be ready to be combined and spooned into the dessert dishes.)

30 minutes before serving:

Prepare the Garlic Bread.

15 minutes before serving:

Prepare the spaghetti according to package
  instructions.

5 minutes before serving:

Combine the salad with the watercress.

Shopping List

Stock Items

___ Garlic
___ Marjoram
___ Salt
___ Garlic powder
___ Almond extract
___ Vegetable oil or
       bacon drippings
___ Red wine vinegar
___ Parmesan cheese
___ Powdered sugar

___ Basil
___ Parsley
___ Pepper
___ Thyme
___ Vanilla
___ Olive oil
___ Butter
___ Burgundy or red
       cooking wine

Special Purchases

___ 1 medium onion
___ 2 medium red onions
___ 3 medium cucumbers
___ 3 medium tomatoes
___ 3 bunches watercress
___ 2 large cans Italian-style plum tomatoes, whole

___ 2 small cans tomato paste (6 ounces each)
___ 1 small can tomato puree
___ 1½ pounds ground beef or Italian sausage
___ 1 pound package spaghetti (or other pasta)
___ 1 large loaf French bread, not sliced
___ 2½ cups whipping cream
___ Italian macaroons
___ Sliced almonds

🕭 *Spaghetti Sauce* 🕭

1 medium onion
5 cloves garlic
2 tablespoons vegetable oil or bacon drippings
2 large cans Italian-style plum tomatoes
2 small (6-ounce) cans of tomato paste
1 teaspoon basil
1 teaspoon marjoram
1 teaspoon parsley
1 teaspoon salt
½ teaspoon pepper
1½ cups burgundy or red cooking wine
1½ pounds meat, either ground beef, Italian
    sausage, or a combination
1 pound of spaghetti (pasta) prepared according
    to package directions
Grated cheese

Chop the onion and mince the garlic.

In a large pot, heat the vegetable oil or bacon drippings. Add the onion and garlic and cook over medium heat until the onion is transparent and soft. Add the tomatoes and tomato paste and stir to blend. Add all the remaining ingredients, except the meat, pasta, and cheese. Stir to blend and simmer over low heat 1–3 hours.

In the last hour of cooking, brown the meat in a large frying pan over medium-high heat. Stir the meat and break up the chunks as it cooks. Once the meat is nicely browned on all sides, drain it on several layers of paper towels. Then add the meat to the sauce and stir to blend. Continue to simmer for at least 30 more minutes.

Serve the sauce over the hot spaghetti and pass the Parmesan cheese separately.

❦ *Garlic Bread* ❦

Preheat oven to 300 degrees.

1 large loaf of French bread, not sliced
1 stick butter
Garlic powder
Grated Parmesan cheese

Cut the French bread into 1-inch thick slices but do not cut it all the way through; the slices should all be attached at the bottom. Using your fingers, separate each slice of bread and drop in a slice of butter, a couple good shakes of garlic powder, and a couple good shakes of Parmesan cheese. Repeat this procedure for all of the slices. Wrap the bread in aluminum foil and heat in the 300-degree oven for 20 minutes.

🍂 *Almond Cream* 🍂

6 pairs of dry Italian macaroons, crushed, approx-
    imately 1 cup (the kind that come in the red
    tin, or something similar)
½ cup powdered sugar
Pinch of salt
2½ cups whipping cream

½ teaspoon almond extract
1½ teaspoons vanilla
¼ cup sliced, toasted almonds (To toast the almonds,
    spread them out on a plate or cookie sheet and
    place under the broiler for a couple of minutes.
    As they start to brown, remove them from the
    broiler, stir them around and return to the
    broiler just until they are a light golden color.)

In a medium bowl, combine the macaroon crumbs,
sugar, salt and 1¼ cups of the cream (be sure not to
use all of the cream, just 1¼ cups). Stir to blend.
Cover with plastic wrap and refrigerate for 30–45
minutes, until the macaroons are soft.

In a small bowl, whip the remaining 1¼ cups whipping cream until soft peaks form. Add the almond
extract and the vanilla and continue beating until
the cream is stiff. Fold the cream mixture into
the macaroon mixture and spoon into small dessert
dishes. Cover each dish and freeze the Almond
Cream for about 2 hours before serving.

To serve, remove Almond Cream from the freezer
and top with toasted almonds.

❧ *Tomato, Onion, and Cucumber Salad* ❧

3 medium cucumbers, peeled, halved lengthwise, and thinly sliced

¼ teaspoon salt

6 tablespoons olive oil

2 medium red onions, thinly sliced

3 cloves garlic, crushed

3 tomatoes, chopped

3 tablespoons tomato puree

3 tablespoons red wine vinegar

½ teaspoon dried thyme

½ teaspoon dried basil

½ teaspoon freshly ground pepper

3 bunches of watercress, cleaned and trimmed (If you are not familiar with watercress, ask someone in the produce department of your local store to show it to you and show you how to trim it. It is a light-tasting, small-leafed green. Trimming it mainly involves removing the heavy stems.)

Place the sliced cucumbers in a small saucepan and cover with water. Add 1–2 pinches of salt and bring to a boil over medium-high heat. Boil for 2 minutes. The cucumbers should be soft with a slight bit of crispness but not mushy.

Drain the cucumber in a colander or strainer. Spread the cucumbers out on paper towels to allow them to dry completely.

Using a medium frying pan, heat the oil over medium low heat. Add the onion and garlic and cook, stirring regularly until the onion has softened, about 5 minutes. Remove the pan from the heat and combine all the remaining ingredients except the watercress. Refrigerate until you are ready to serve, at least one hour or up to 6 hours.

To serve, place the cleaned and trimmed watercress in the bottom of the individual bowls. Top with the tomato, onion, and cucumber mixture. The oil and vinegar in the mixture forms the dressing for the salads.

Kids' Helps

Spaghetti Sauce: Once you have chopped up the onion and garlic, let the children add them to the pot and stir while they cook. Kids can continue stirring as you add the tomatoes, tomato paste, and seasonings.

Garlic Bread: Have one child help you by holding the slices of bread apart from one another while you or another child add the butter, garlic powder, and cheese.

Almond Cream: While the macaroons are still in the paper wrapping, have the children hold them over the bowl and crush them. After you have added the sugar, salt, and cream they can stir the mixture until it is blended. They can whip the cream using the electric beater, and with your help they can fold the whipped cream into the macaroon mixture.

Tomato, Onion, and Cucumber Salad: Children can help with this salad by stirring the onion and garlic as they cook.

Old-Fashioned Thanksgiving Dinner

Cranberry-Orange Relish
Old-Fashioned Roast Turkey
Brussels Sprouts with
Garlic Cream Sauce
Four Vegetable Puree
Perfect Pumpkin Pie

Everyone dreams of the perfect Thanksgiving dinner. The aroma of turkey stuffed with perfect stuffing like grandma used to make wafting through the house, the fragrant selection of fall vegetables, and of course, the pumpkin pie.

I remember my grandmother always made a cranberry-orange relish for Thanksgiving. The one in this menu isn't her exact recipe but it always reminds me of the security of a family Thanksgiving. When you see how easy this recipe is, you'll wonder why anyone ever buys canned cranberry sauce.

You can have that perfect dinner without going to grandma's and without being in New England. In fact *you* could invite grandma over, make the Old-Fashioned Turkey Dinner, and top it off with the Perfect Pumpkin Pie. This menu offers all the parts you'll need without being so full of extra work that you'll have to start on it a week ahead.

With a meal as terrific as this one you won't want to wait for it once a year. Why not serve it frequently? Next time your local grocery store has whole fresh turkeys on sale for a great price, pick one up. They will keep uncooked in the refrigerator for up to a week. Keep it until Sunday and make a special "Sunday for giving thanks" dinner. You will have wonderful leftovers for the following week.

Timetable

1–3 days before serving:
Prepare the Cranberry-Orange Relish.

The night before serving:
Make the Perfect Pumpkin Pie.

3½ hours before serving:
Prepare stuffing and turkey.

3 hours before serving:
Stuff the turkey.
Put the turkey in the oven.

2½ hours before serving:
Prepare all the vegetables and set aside.

½ hour before serving:
Boil the carrots, turnips, and rutabagas.
Boil the brussels sprouts.

20 minutes before serving:

Puree the carrots, turnips, and rutabagas.

15 minutes before serving:

Prepare Garlic Cream Sauce for the brussels sprouts.

10 minutes before serving:

Remove turkey from the oven and cut the bag. Place the turkey on a serving platter.

5 minutes before serving:

Make the gravy.

Shopping List

Stock Items

___ Sugar
___ Unbaked pie shell
___ Eggs
___ Flour
___ Nutmeg
___ Pepper
___ Parsley
___ Basil

___ Ginger
___ Brown sugar
___ Butter
___ Cinnamon
___ Salt
___ Milk
___ Tarragon
___ Whole garlic

Special Purchases

___ 1 orange
___ 1 bag fresh or frozen cranberries
___ 1 large bag pecan pieces
___ 1 16-ounce can solid-pack pumpkin
___ 3 8-ounce cartons whipping cream

___ 1 11–13 pound turkey
___ 2 6-ounce packages cornbread stuffing mix
___ 3 onions; 2 large, 1 medium
___ Celery
___ 1 8-ounce can water chestnuts
___ 1 can chicken broth
___ 12 brussels sprouts
___ 2 medium turnips
___ 2 medium rutabagas
___ 1 pound carrots
___ Reynolds Oven Cooking Bag—turkey size
___ Kitchen Bouquet

❦ *Cranberry-Orange Relish* ❦

¾ cup sugar
Grated orange peel of 1 orange
Fresh-squeezed juice of 1 orange (this may be
    the same orange)
¼ teaspoon ginger powder
1 12-ounce bag fresh or fresh/frozen cranberries
1 handful of chopped pecans, toasted

To toast the pecans, place them on a cookie sheet or piece of aluminum foil and toast under the broiler or in the toaster oven for approximately 3 minutes. Pecans should be lightly browned but not black.

Combine everything except the cranberries and pecans in a medium saucepan and bring to a gentle boil over medium heat. Stir frequently until the sugar dissolves. Add the cranberries and cook until the berries begin to pop, stirring occasionally (approximately 5 minutes). Stir in the toasted pecans. Pour the Cranberry-Orange Relish into a pretty serving bowl, cover, and refrigerate until you are ready to use.

🥜 *Perfect Pumpkin Pie* 🥜

Preheat oven to 400 degrees.

1 unbaked pie shell (See Marita's Pie Crust, page 174.)

Filling
1 16-ounce can solid-pack pumpkin (not pumpkin pie mix)
1 cup brown sugar
2 eggs
2 tablespoons butter, melted
1 tablespoon flour
1 teaspoon ground ginger
1 teaspoon cinnamon
½ teaspoon freshly grated nutmeg
½ teaspoon salt
½ teaspoon freshly grated pepper
¾ cup milk
¾ cup whipping cream

Mix everything except the milk and cream in a large bowl and stir until they are well blended. Add the milk and cream. Stir until the entire mixture is well blended and has an even color. Pour the filling into the pie shell. Bake in the preheated oven at 400 degrees for 1 hour and 10 minutes. When the pie is done it will be evenly risen and the center will be fairly firm when it is shaken. To serve, cut the pie into 6 even wedges and top with Whipped Cream Topping.

Whipped Cream Topping

1 cup whipping cream
1 teaspoon vanilla
1 tablespoon sugar

Using an electric beater, beat the whipping cream in a medium bowl until it forms soft peaks. (It will make a slight mound when the beaters are lifted out. Beater must be turned off before you check this.) Add the vanilla and sugar and beat just until they are blended.

❧ *Old-Fashioned Roast Turkey* ❧

Preheat the oven to 350 degrees.

1 11–13 pound fresh turkey
Salt and pepper
2 6-ounce packages cornbread stuffing mix
2 sticks butter
1 large onion
4 stalks celery
1 8-ounce can sliced water chestnuts
1 cup chicken broth
1 tablespoon fresh parsley, snipped into small pieces
1 teaspoon tarragon
1 teaspoon basil
¾ cup pecan pieces

Reynolds Oven Cooking Bag for turkey
1 tablespoon flour
1 large onion
4 stalks celery

3 tablespoons flour

Remove the neck and giblets from the inside of the turkey. Rinse the inside and outside of the turkey with cold water. Using paper towels, pat the turkey dry. Set aside.

In a large pot or dutch oven, melt the butter over medium heat. If the butter starts to brown, remove from the heat until the vegetables are added. Meanwhile, peel and chop the onion and slice the celery. Add the onion and celery to the melted butter. Drain the water from the water chestnuts and add them to the celery-onion mixture. Cook until the celery and onions are soft. Add the freshly snipped parsley, the tarragon, and the basil. Add the cornbread stuffing mix and pecans. Stir to blend. Add the chicken stock and stir to blend. Season to taste with salt and pepper.

Lightly stuff the body and neck cavities of the turkey with the stuffing. Do not overpack the stuffing. There will be some stuffing left over. Close up the openings with the loose turkey skin and toothpicks or skewers.

Put 1 tablespoon of flour inside the cooking bag. Close the bag and shake it to dust the inside of the bag with flour. Sprinkle the inside of the bag with salt and pepper. Peel and slice the onion. Slice the celery. Holding the bag on its side, place the onion and celery in the bottom of the bag. Place the turkey inside the bag, on top of the vegetables. Close the bag with the fastener that is provided with the bag. Make 6 ½-inch slits in the top of the bag. The part of the bag being fastened should be at the end of the turkey, not on the top like a sack of trash. Place the turkey and bag in a roasting pan and put in the preheated oven 2–2½ hours.

When the turkey is finished cooking, remove it from the oven. Cut the bag open and carefully lift the turkey to a serving platter. Save the pan drippings for the gravy.

To make the gravy, put 3 tablespoons of pan drippings into a medium saucepan over medium heat. Add 3 tablespoons of flour and stir to form a thick paste. Add the remaining pan drippings ¼ cup at a time and stir after each addition. Do not add the remaining pan juices until the first ¼ cup is well blended and the gravy has thickened. Once it has thickened, add the next ¼ cup and repeat the process until all the pan drippings are used. A few drops of Kitchen Bouquet may be used to deepen the color of the gravy.

❦ Brussels Sprouts with Garlic Cream Sauce ❦

12 brussels sprouts
½ teaspoon salt

2 tablespoons butter
2 medium cloves garlic, finely chopped
½ cup whipping cream
½ teaspoon salt
Freshly ground pepper

Clean brussels sprouts by trimming the ends and removing all the damaged and tough-looking leaves. The part you use should look like a perfect little baby cabbage.

Cook the brussels sprouts in a medium pot of boiling salted water for about 10 minutes or until they are just barely tender. Remove them from the heat and rinse under cold water to stop the cooking process. Drain the water.

In a large saucepan, melt the butter over medium-high heat. Add the garlic and cook until the garlic is softened. Do not brown. Add the cream, salt, and pepper and bring to a gentle boil. Continue boiling until the mixture thickens slightly. Add the brussels sprouts and stir them until they are fully coated with the cream mixture. Serve 2 brussels sprouts per person and top with remaining cream sauce.

❦ *Four Vegetable Puree* ❦

1 medium onion, peeled and cut into eighths
2 medium turnips, peeled and cut into eighths
2 medium rutabagas, peeled and cut into eighths
1 pound carrots, peeled and cut into 1-inch pieces
6 cloves garlic, peeled

½ stick butter
Salt
Freshly ground pepper
Freshly grated nutmeg

In a large pot of boiling water, cook all the vegetables until they are tender, about 15 minutes. Drain the water.

Using the food processor, puree the vegetables in batches until they are all smooth. Return pureed vegetables to the pot and heat until any excess liquid is absorbed. Season to taste with the salt and pepper. The Four Vegetable Puree should be about the consistency of mashed potatoes. Serve topped with a little freshly grated nutmeg.

Kids' Helps

Cranberry-Orange Relish: The children can stir the sugar, orange peel, orange juice, and ginger mixture over the heat until the sugar dissolves. They can pour the cranberries into the hot mixture and continue stirring until the berries begin to pop. They can continue stirring while you add the toasted pecans.

Perfect Pumpkin Pie: Since the ingredients for the pie are simply stirred together, kids can help by stirring and adding premeasured ingredients. For the whipped topping they can whip the cream using an electric beater.

Old-Fashioned Roast Turkey: In making the stuffing, children can help by adding the vegetables to the pot and stirring while you continue to chop the remaining vegetables. After the cornbread stuffing mix has been added, the stuffing will probably be too stiff for little ones to stir. Their extra hands will be very helpful when you put the turkey into the cooking bag. Have them hold the bag open while you place the turkey inside.

Brussels Sprouts with Garlic Cream Sauce: Have children stir the garlic while it cooks.

Four Vegetable Puree: Children can help puree the vegetables by turning the food processor on and off.

❦ Christmas ❦ Dinner

**Crisp Salad with
Cider Dressing
Classic Prime Rib
Roast Potatoes
Yorkshire Pudding
Broccoli Almondine
English Trifle**

Serves 6

You will want to have this Classic Prime Rib and English Yorkshire Pudding meal more than once a year but its dessert of English Trifle and the overall formal fare lends itself perfectly to a festive family dinner. My father's family had a prime rib dinner every Sunday afternoon and it became a contest to see who would get the prized end cuts. In my childhood we had prime rib only for special occasions like Christmas and birthdays. Most children might prefer hamburgers or hot dogs but when my birthday came around and my mother asked me what I wanted for my birthday dinner, I usually chose prime rib. Now in my own home it has become a favorite again. When I ask Chuck what he would like for dinner, he often requests "that prime rib you make with the Yorkshire pudding." Since it takes several hours to cook and some advance planning to get the right cut of beef, Chuck usually doesn't get his wish fulfilled. But for Christmas and special occasions the advance planning and extra shopping prove to be well worth the effort.

For a meal this special, don't scrimp. Buy the best beef you can get. This will usually mean going to a special meat market rather than your grocery store's meat department (since most stores today save you money by offering lower quality ungraded meats). For this meal try to find a standing rib roast that is graded "prime."

Unfortunately most of the "prime" beef goes to restaurants and the best you may be able to find is "choice." Choice is perfectly acceptable and will make an excellent roast but don't settle for anything less than "choice."

Once you have selected the beef the rest is easy, even cooking the prime rib. If you have not had Yorkshire pudding before, it will surprise you. The surprise is that it is not pudding at all, but rather something like a cross between crackers and bread. The English Trifle is the biggest surprise of all. I got the recipe from an English friend of mine who was forced to find a substitute for the traditional lady fingers one day when her local market was out of them. The result is this beautiful, traditional creation made with Twinkies! This is the only time you will find me suggesting something as prepackaged as Twinkies. It really goes against my grain but you'll find, as my friend and I did, that the Twinkies really make a great presentation.

If you are having guests other than those who live in your house, this would be an excellent time to allow them to bring something. When they ask, "Can I bring anything?" tell them you have an excellent salad that they could prepare and that you will send them the recipe. The English Trifle is the other part that is easy to ask someone else to do. Both the salad and the trifle need to be made ahead so your guests won't be laboring over their tasks as they rush out the door. In addition both the salad and the trifle take up quite a bit of refrigerator space and with the large roast in there, you may run out of room until the roast is in the oven.

So deck the halls and treat your family and friends to this elegant and easy Christmas feast!

Timetable

The evening before serving:

Prepare the salad greens.
Prepare the English Trifle.

3 hours before serving:

Prepare and cook the Classic Prime Rib.

2¹/₂ hours before serving:

Prepare the salad dressing and set aside.

45 minutes before serving:

Place the cake pan in the oven with the bacon fat.
Prepare the English Yorkshire Pudding batter.
Reheat the salad dressing and add the apple to
  the salad.

30 minutes before serving:

Increase the oven heat and place the English Yorkshire Pudding in the oven.

Toss and serve the salad.

15 minutes before serving:

Allow your guests to continue to enjoy their salads.

Remove the prime rib from the oven.

Prepare the broccoli.

To serve:

Remove the salad plates from the table and arrange
the Classic Prime Rib with Roast Potatoes, English
Yorkshire Pudding, and Broccoli Almondine on each
plate and serve.

Shopping List

Stock Items

___ Vegetable oil
___ Nutmeg
___ Pepper
___ Brown sugar
___ Milk
___ Butter
___ Bacon fat

___ Cider vinegar
___ Salt
___ Garlic cloves
___ Flour
___ Eggs
___ Bacon

Special Purchases

___ 1 6–8 pound standing rib roast
___ 8 large shallots
___ ½ pound Jicama
___ 4 heads Belgian endive

___ 1 large head red lettuce
___ 1 head curly endive
___ 1 large bunch green onions
___ 1 large Granny Smith apple
___ 2 large onions
___ 12 small red potatoes
___ 2–2½ pounds of broccoli
___ Lemon
___ Fresh strawberries
___ Unsweetened apple cider
___ Red wine
___ Blanched, slivered almonds
___ Twinkies
___ Apricot jam
___ Bird's Imported Dessert Mix
___ 1 8-ounce carton whipping cream
___ Chocolate sprinkles
___ Nuts
___ Cherries

❧ *Crisp Salad with Cider Dressing* ❧

You may have noticed that I am not a big salad fan. I believe in making a meal balanced but easy. When you already have fresh vegetables I don't see a big need for the extra fuss of salad. But in the case of a formal meal like this one, a fresh and unique salad seems appropriate. I suggest that you try this one once before the big day, not because it is difficult to make but so you will be sold on its value too.

15 thin slices of bacon
⅓ cup vegetable oil

8 large shallots
3 cups unsweetened apple cider
4 tablespoons cider vinegar
2 teaspoons brown sugar
¼ teaspoon freshly grated nutmeg
Freshly ground pepper

½ pound Jicama
4 heads Belgian endive
1 large head red lettuce
1 head curly endive
1 bunch large green onions (approximately 6)

1 large Granny Smith apple

In the microwave, on the microwave bacon cooker, cook the bacon in 2 batches until it is crisp, 6–8 minutes per batch. If you don't have a microwave bacon cooker, cook the bacon the way you usually do. Save 2 tablespoons of the bacon fat for the dressing. Transfer the cooked bacon to paper towels to absorb any remaining fat. Chop the cooked bacon into ½-inch pieces and scoop all the bacon, including the little crumbly pieces, into a small bowl. Set aside.

In a small saucepan, bring the cider to a boil and continue boiling until the cider is reduced to about ⅓ cup.

Meanwhile, peel and thinly slice the shallots. In a large frying pan over medium heat, heat the remaining 2 tablespoons of bacon fat with the vegetable oil. Add the shallots, cook and stir frequently until they are golden brown, about 15 minutes. Add the ⅓ cup reduced cider, the vinegar, and the sugar and simmer 1 minute. Add the nutmeg and a generous amount of pepper. Remove from heat and set aside.

Peel the Jicama and cut into 1½-inch pieces that resemble thick matchsticks. Cut the Belgian endive into ½-inch wide slices. Tear the red lettuce and the curly endive into bite-size pieces. Trim the roots and darker green stem from the green onions. Diagonally slice remaining green onion into thin slices. Combine the Jicama, Belgian endive, red lettuce, curly endive, and green onion in a large salad bowl. Cover with plastic wrap and refrigerate.

Just before serving, core the apple (do not peel) and cut into matchstick pieces. Toss into the salad.

Bring the dressing to a boil over medium heat and pour over the mixed greens. Toss the salad well to be sure that it is evenly coated with the dressing.

To serve, divide the salad among the salad plates and top with the crumbled bacon.

❧ *Classic Prime Rib with Roast Potatoes* ❧

This is a great main course to make. It is very simple to prepare but is always impressive because almost no one ever cooks it at home. As you can see there is almost nothing to it but a little advance planning.

Preheat the oven to 325 degrees.

1 6–8 pound standing rib roast, prime or choice (the
 small end is the best)
2 large cloves garlic
2 large onions
salt
pepper

1½ cups dry red wine, red cooking wine, or cabernet
 sauvignon
12 small red potatoes

If needed trim the fat so that only ¼ inch of fat
remains. Place the meat bone-side down in a roasting pan that is slightly larger than the meat. Cut the
garlic in half and rub the entire surface of the meat
with the garlic halves. Leave the garlic in the pan.
Slice both onions, one into thin slices and the other
4 or 5 thicker slices. Lay the thin slices around the
meat in the roasting pan. Place the thicker onion
slices on the top and sides of the meat and hold them
in place with wooden toothpicks. Generously sprinkle the meat with salt and pepper. Insert the meat
thermometer into the center of the meat. Thermometer must not be touching the bone.

Place the meat in the oven and roast. Every 20–30
minutes baste the meat by pouring about ⅓ cup of
wine over the meat. When the wine is used up, continue basting the meat throughout the remaining
cooking time by using the pan juices. Lift up one
corner of the pan so all the juices go into another
corner and spoon them over the top.

Continue cooking until the meat thermometer reads 140 degrees for rare or 160 degrees for medium (about 20–22 minutes of cooking time per pound for rare and 24–27 minutes per pound for medium).

Peel 1 strip around the potatoes so the ends are still red and the centers are white. (This is just for decoration, if you prefer you may peel the entire potato or leave them entirely unpeeled.) Bring a medium pot of water to a boil over medium-high heat. Sprinkle the water with salt. Add the potatoes and boil for 10 minutes. During the last 45 minutes of the meat's cooking time, place the potatoes in the roasting pan around the roast and turn them once to coat them with the pan juices. During the remaining cooking time turn the potatoes at least once.

To serve cut the prime rib into ½–1-inch thick slices and place on the dinner plate with 2 potatoes. Spoon some of the pan juices over each piece of meat. Traditionally the men get the thicker slices with the bone and the women get the slices in between.

🦌 *English Yorkshire Pudding* 🦌

If you are baking English Yorkshire Pudding to serve with the Prime Rib and you only have one oven you are presented with a problem since they need to be cooked at different temperatures. You have several options. One is to invite your next door neighbors and use their oven. If you prefer to keep Christmas a family affair it is okay to raise the temperature on the roast at the very end. Since the roast needs to stand out of the oven for about 15 minutes before carving and the Yorkshire Pudding needs to be served as soon as it comes out of the oven, there is only about 15 minutes of time when they are in the oven together and it will work fine. The Yorkshire Pudding needs a hot oven to cook so be sure to remove the Prime Rib quickly so the oven door is open as little as possible.

Preheat the oven to 400 degrees (unless it already has the meat in it—then raise it to 375 degrees just before the Yorkshire Pudding goes in).

¾ cup flour
¼ teaspoon salt
1 cup milk (if using whole milk rather than low-fat milk use half milk and half water)
1 egg
1 tablespoon bacon fat or butter

Place the bacon fat in a square cake pan and put it in the oven for 15 minutes to melt the fat and heat the pan.

Combine all of the ingredients in a blender and mix on high until they are smooth and foamy. Set them in the refrigerator until the pan is ready. Once the pan has been heated for 15 minutes remove it from the oven and pour the batter into it. Quickly return the pan to the oven. Adjust the temperature if needed. Cook for 30 minutes or until the top is golden brown and the edges are puffy. To serve, cut into squares and place a piece on each plate next to the meat.

❧ *Broccoli Almondine* ❧

2–2½ pounds broccoli
Salt
Freshly ground black pepper
Juice of ½ lemon
⅓ cup blanched, slivered almonds
4 tablespoons butter
1 clove finely chopped garlic

Trim the broccoli into nice little clusters and place in the top of the microwave vegetable steamer. Place a couple tablespoons of water in the bottom of the steamer, add the top part and cover. Cook in the microwave on high 6–8 minutes. Meanwhile, melt the butter in a small frying pan over medium heat. Add the almonds and the garlic and cook until the almonds are lightly browned, about 5 minutes.

To serve, place the broccoli on the plates, sprinkle with juice, salt, and pepper, and top with the almond-garlic mixture.

❧ *English Trifle* ❧

This item is a favorite of mine. It doesn't need to be cooked, all of the ingredients are interchangeable, and the amounts don't matter too much. You can just use whatever you have as long as the ingredients are remotely similar to the ones I am suggesting.

Twinkies, regular or fruit filled, approximately
    1 box (The amount will vary depending on
    the size of your bowl.)

Apricot jam, regular-size jar (You may use any other
  flavor jam you have available.)
1 envelope Bird's Imported Dessert Mix or Jello
  vanilla pudding mix, made according to
  package instructions
1 pint fresh strawberries (You may substitute any
  other fresh or frozen fruit.)
1 cup whipping cream, whipped
Chocolate sprinkles, nuts, cherries

Use a trifle bowl or a large clear glass bowl. Your
bowl size will determine the quantity of the ingredients. Slice the Twinkies in half lengthwise. Line
the bowl with the Twinkies, filling side out. Use
enough of the remaining Twinkies to cover the bottom of the bowl with bite-size pieces. Heat the jar of
jam in the microwave or in a pot of boiling water
until it is semifluid. Brush the jam on the Twinkies
and dab the remaining jam on the bottom. Pour the
pudding over the Twinkies and the jam to 1–2 inches
thick. Next add the strawberries or other fruit to
1–2 inches thick. Top with the whipped cream and
garnish with nuts, sprinkles, and halved cherries.
Refrigerate for at least 3 hours and not more than 24.
Custard and whipped cream may be flavored with a
few teaspoons of flavoring such as almond extract or
Grand Marnier, if desired.

Kids' Helps

Crisp Salad with Cider Dressing: Children can help
with this salad by stirring the shallots while they are

cooking. Just before serving they can sprinkle the salads with the crumbled bacon.

Classic Prime Rib with Roast Potatoes: Once you have cut the clove of garlic in half, let the children rub the cut side of the garlic over the surface of the meat. They can generously sprinkle the meat with salt and pepper. When you are ready to cook the potatoes, have the older children peel the potatoes.

English Yorkshire Pudding: Once all the ingredients are in the blender, let the kids turn it on until the batter is smooth and foamy.

Broccoli Almondine: Children can help with this recipe by stirring the almond garlic mixture as it cooks.

English Trifle: Kids will love to help with this item since the basis for the trifle is Twinkies. Once you have cut the Twinkies in half, let the children carefully place them in the bowl with the cream side facing out. Cover the bottom with bite-size pieces. Be aware that they will be apt to sneak a piece or two. Since the jar of jam may be heavy and too hot for little ones you may need to brush the Twinkies with the jam and add the pudding. Then let the children add the fruit. They can whip the cream and spoon it on top. Let them sprinkle the chocolate sprinkles on top and place the cherries halves where they think they should go.

🍎 *Easter Sunday* 🍎 *Dinner*

Easter Ham
Candied Carrots
Rice Pilaf
Lemon Meringue Pie

Serves 8

Easter is a very special day. It commemorates the fact that Christ has risen from the dead and has given us new life. It comes at a time when the earth is coming to life again and everything seems fresh and new. I remember my sister and I always got special Easter dresses with new shoes and matching gloves. We went to church in our new frilly finery. After church we went home for the festivities. Several families were usually invited to join us and all the children, similarly clad in the best of the season, searched our backyard for the eggs we had so carefully colored just a few days before. With our baskets full of colored eggs and sparkling chocolates, our cheeks rosy with excitement and the sun glistening in our hair, we would follow the fragrance of Easter dinner into the house and settle down for a favorite dinner: the Easter Ham.

With the yellow and purple of the Easter eggs and the pastel colors of pretty dresses a pink ham seems so appropriate! There is no easier feast to prepare than a baked ham. You almost *can't* do it wrong. In fact I don't know that you can. My mother tells me that when I was a little girl I turned up the oven when the ham was in it, as high as it would go. No one noticed until it was time to serve. There in the center of the oven was a black ham! This was before blackened food was trendy. She claims that it was one of the best hams ever. Crispy on the outside with the juices sealed in on the inside. While I am not going to suggest cooking your ham at 500 degrees, I doubt that you would come up with a bad ham no matter what you did.

In this version of Easter Sunday Dinner I have included a recipe like the ham my mother used to make before she gave up cooking; a basic ham studded with cloves and basted throughout the cooking time with a brown sugar and mustard glaze. With this dinner, a vegetable with a sweet touch is appropriate. My mother always served a casserole of canned apple pie filling and canned yams with brown sugar and butter on top. While I loved that dish as a child, it seems a bit too much for today's fresher and lighter eating styles. Instead I've suggested a favorite vegetable from my grandmother's house, Candied Carrots. They have a sweet touch, are fresh, and give a nice color to the Easter dinner plate. With the glazed ham and the Candied Carrots, the starch should be light. A buttery Rice Pilaf fits the meal perfectly. To top off this colorful menu I suggest Lemon Meringue Pie. The yellow color fits in with the Easter scheme and the fluffy meringue adds to the lightness of the meal.

This is a meal you will want more often than once a year. Since everything involved in making this festive feast is available all year long, why wait for Easter? Celebrate our risen Lord anytime. Christ is risen indeed!

Timetable

3 hours before serving:
Score the ham.
Prepare the glaze.

2½ hours before serving:
Place ham in the oven.
Prepare the Lemon Meringue Pie.

2 hours before serving:
Take a rest!

35 minutes before serving:
Prepare the Rice Pilaf.

15 minutes before serving:
Prepare the carrots.

Shopping List

Stock Items

___ Brown sugar
___ Cornstarch
___ Dried minced onion
    flakes
___ Pepper

___ Sugar
___ Dried parsley flakes
___ Salt
___ Chicken bouillon
    cubes

___ Eggs   ___ Butter

___ Bacon fat   ___ Prepared mustard

Special Purchases

___ ½ ham, butt portion

___ 12 medium carrots

___ 3 lemons

___ Vermicelli

___ White rice, blue rose type

___ 1 9-inch pie crust

❦ *Easter Ham* ❦

Preheat oven to 325 degrees.

½ fully cooked ham, butt portion (usually 6–8
    pounds)
Whole cloves
½ cup brown sugar
½ cup prepared mustard
3 tablespoons melted bacon fat

Score the fatty portion of the ham to create a diamond-shaped pattern with the diamonds being about 1 inch across. Place a clove, pointed side down, into the fat of each diamond shape. Place the ham, fat side facing up, in a roasting pan.

In a small bowl combine the brown sugar, mustard, and bacon fat. Brush the ham with the glaze, coating the fat and the meaty sides with a light coating of glaze. (There will be quite a bit of glaze left.) Place the ham in the oven and cook 2–2½ hours. Brush the ham with more glaze every half-hour or until there is no more glaze.

If you are serving a larger crowd and are using a whole ham, score the fatty covering just as for the half ham, double the glaze, and cook 12–15 minutes per pound.

🍓 *Candied Carrots* 🍓

12 medium carrots
2 tablespoons butter
2 tablespoons brown sugar

Trim and peel or clean the carrots. Slice them into 1/3-inch thick slices and place the sliced carrots in the top portion of a microwave vegetable steamer. Place a couple of tablespoons of water in the bottom of the steamer, add the top portion, and cover. Cook on high in the microwave for 8 minutes or until carrots reach the desired tenderness. Pour the water out of the bottom portion. Empty the cooked carrots into the bottom portion of the microwave vegetable steamer. Add the butter and brown sugar. Replace the cover and shake the steamer until the carrots are fully covered with the butter and brown sugar. Serve.

🍓 *Rice Pilaf* 🍓

An Armenian friend from Fresno, California, first introduced me to rice pilaf. I loved it so much I asked her to show me how to make it. I have since lost her real recipe but I think she would be happy with my adaptation.

8 tablespoons butter (1½ sticks)
2 coils of dry, uncooked vermicelli (A fine spaghetti-like pasta that comes in a coil which slightly resembles a bird's nest. There are several coils per package.)
2 cups white rice, not the quick cooking kind
4 cups water
2 chicken bouillon cubes
1 tablespoon dried parsley
1 tablespoon minced onion flakes
1 teaspoon salt
Freshly ground pepper

Using a large saucepan, melt the butter over medium heat. Break the coils of vermicelli into little pieces and add them to the melted butter. Cook until the vermicelli has a nice golden color, stirring frequently, about 5 minutes. Add the rice and stir until the rice is nicely coated with butter, about 2 minutes. Add the remaining ingredients and stir to blend. Reduce the heat to low. Cover the pan and cook over low heat until all the liquid is absorbed, about 25 minutes. Stir a couple of times throughout the cooking time. Fluff the rice with a fork before serving.

❦ *Lemon Meringue Pie* ❦

Preheat oven to 350 degrees.

1 cooked pie crust (See Marita's Pie Crust on page 174.)

Filling:

1½ cups sugar
7 tablespoons cornstarch
A dash of salt
1½ cups water
3 beaten egg yolks
Grated peel of 1 lemon
2 tablespoons butter
½ cup lemon juice

Using a medium saucepan, combine the sugar, corn-starch, and salt. Stir well, to the point that the corn-starch is completely mixed in with the sugar. Stir in the water. Bring the mixture to a boil over medium heat and cook until the mixture thickens and is translucent, stirring continuously. Remove the pan from the heat and stir a small amount (about 1 table-spoon) of the sugar mixture into the egg yolks. Pour all of the egg yolk mixture into the sugar mixture. Return the pan to the heat and bring to a boil, stir-ring continuously. Once the mixture comes to a boil, remove it from the heat. Stir in the butter. Once the butter has melted and blended, stir in the lemon peel. Set the mixture aside to cool. Stir it occasion-ally to prevent a film from forming on the top.

Meringue

4 egg whites
1 teaspoon lemon juice
6 tablespoons sugar

Using an electric mixer, beat the egg whites and the lemon juice together until soft peaks form. Continue beating and add the sugar, 1 tablespoon at a time until all the sugar has dissolved and the egg whites form stiff peaks.

Pour the lemon filling into the pie crust. Top the filling with the egg whites. Spread the egg whites to the edge of the pastry. Using a spoon, create peaks and valleys in the meringue.

Bake 12–15 minutes or until the meringue is golden brown. (If you are cooking the pie at the same time as the ham, turn up the oven temperature for the 15 minutes needed to brown the meringue, then return it to 325 degrees.) Allow the pie to cool before serving. Cut into 8 pieces and serve.

Kids' Helps

Easter Ham: Older children can stick the cloves into the diamond-pattern cuts you have made in the ham. A younger child can mix the ingredients for the glaze and brush the ham with the glaze before it goes into the oven.

Candied Carrots: Once the carrots are cooked, a child can shake the microwave steamer to coat the carrots with the sugar and butter.

Rice Pilaf: Have a child stir the vermicelli until it is lightly browned. Add the rice and have the child continue stirring while you add the remaining ingredients.

Lemon meringue Pie: Once all the dry ingredients are in the saucepan, let a child stir them until they are fully blended. Let the child continue stirring while you add the water and the mixture cooks. After you have mixed a small amount of the sugar mixture into the egg yolks, let the child stir while you pour all of the egg yolks into the saucepan and continue to stir while the mixture comes to a boil. This recipe involves a lot of stirring, so several children may need to take turns. They are apt to need lots of encouragement at this point. Let them drop in the butter pieces while you stir the mixture to blend in the butter. For the meringue, once you have separated the eggs, let the children take turns beating the egg whites using the electric beater. Once the egg whites have formed soft peaks, add the sugar and continue to beat the egg whites to form stiff peaks.

🍎 ***Mother's Day*** 🍎

Special Breakfast
Special Dinner

Serves 4

In some households Mother's Day can be a traumatic event. Dad and the kids want to do something special for Mom, so they either try to cook a special meal or take her out to a restaurant. If Dad is unfamiliar with meal preparation the cooking approach can leave everyone a little testy and the kitchen a disaster that Mom eventually has to clean up. A trip to a restaurant can be equally frustrating. The wait for a table is long, the food is expensive, and the kids get bored.

I surveyed my friends who are mothers, and we concluded that the best approach is to stay home where everyone is comfortable, and to find a meal that Dad and the kids can cook that is both good and simple.

This menu features a simple surprise breakfast that can be prepared before church and a lovely dinner for later in the day.

To start off, Dad needs to check over the shopping list for both menus to see which items are already in the house and which ones he will need to buy before Mother's Day. On the big day itself Dad and the kids need to get up early. Encourage Mom to stay in bed and get some extra rest! Let the kids set the table with the prettiest settings, get out the crystal goblets or stemmed glassware, and even light the candles. Then follow the complete timetable for preparing Homemade Apple Pancakes. Be sure to let the children help so they feel that they are part of this special day.

After church, begin preparations for the Roast Chicken Dinner. This meal provides an easy but elegant dinner that is virtually foolproof and involves a minimum number of steps. Follow the timetable and directions closely for a flawless Mother's Day that is stress-free for both Mom and the family.

If you are not a mother or you don't have a family, or even if you are and you do, these simple menus are appropriate for any time of the year that calls for special meals without a lot of fuss.

Mother's Day Breakfast

Freshly Squeezed Orange Juice
Sausages
Homemade Apple Pancakes

Timetable

30 minutes before serving:

Set the table using your nicest tableware.
Put the butter and syrup on the table.

25 minutes before serving:

Start cooking the sausages.

20 minutes before serving:

Turn on the stove to heat the skillet or griddle.
Prepare the pancake batter.

10 minutes before serving:

Cook the pancakes.

5 minutes before serving:

Pour the freshly squeezed orange juice into the glasses.
Place the glasses on the table.

Shopping List

Stock Items

___ Butter
___ Sugar
___ Baking soda
___ Flour
___ Baking powder
___ Salt

Special Purchases

___ Freshly squeezed orange juice (This can be purchased already squeezed, or you can buy the
oranges and squeeze them yourself. Be sure to
allow extra time if you are going to squeeze
them yourself.)
___ Sausages
___ 2 apples
___ Buttermilk

🐚 *Homemade Apple Pancakes* 🐚
with Fresh Sausages

Serves 4

Sausages (approximately 8)

2 eggs
1½ cups buttermilk
3 tablespoons butter, melted
1½ cups flour
1 tablespoon sugar
1½ teaspoons baking powder
½ teaspoon baking soda
½ teaspoon salt
1 tablespoon lemon juice
2 apples, peeled and grated

In a separate frying pan, cook sausages according to package instructions. Be sure to turn them frequently to keep them evenly browned.

Heat the skillet or griddle over medium heat.

Using a medium-size bowl and the electric beater, beat the eggs on low until they are well blended. Add the buttermilk, melted butter, flour, sugar, baking powder, baking soda, salt, and lemon juice and beat with the electric beater until the mixture is smooth. Add the grated apple and stir with a spoon until it is well blended.

Test the skillet or griddle to check that it is hot enough. Keep your hand high enough above the hot surface to avoid burning (about five inches) and flick a few drops of water off your fingertips onto the hot surface. If the drops bounce and "dance" on the hot surface it is hot enough to cook the pancakes.

Using a large spoon or a ¼ cup measuring cup, pour the batter onto the hot surface. As each pancake spreads it should be about 4 inches in diameter. Be careful to keep the pancakes from touching one another. When the pancakes are puffy and full of bubbles they are ready to be turned over. Once they are turned, cook them for a few more minutes or until they are nicely browned. Serve the pancakes and sausages on individual plates with butter and syrup passed separately.

Kids' Helps

Homemade Apple Pancakes: Let the children set the table using the nicest tableware. If they know how to crack the eggs, let them crack the eggs and empty them into the bowl. They can beat the eggs and then beat the batter after the remaining ingredients have been added. With your guidance the older children can turn the sausages to keep them from browning too heavily on one side, and they can pour the pancake batter onto the cooking surface. When the pancakes are ready to be turned they can flip them over.

Mother's Day Dinner

**Lemon Garlic Roast Chicken
with Potatoes
Table Queen Squash
with Green Peas
Blueberry Buckle**

Serves 4

Timetable

2 hours before serving:

Prepare the chicken.
Peel the potatoes.
Prepare the squash.

1½ hours before serving:

Preheat the oven to 350 degrees.

1¼ hours before serving:

Place the chicken in preheated oven.
Prepare the Blueberry Buckle.

1 hour before serving:

Place the squash and the Blueberry Buckle in the
oven.
Baste the chicken and potatoes.

30 minutes before serving:

Set the table.
Baste the chicken and potatoes.

10 minutes before serving:

Cook the peas according to package instructions.
Baste the chicken and potatoes.
Remove the Blueberry Buckle from the oven and set
   aside.

To serve:

Using the poultry shears, cut the chicken into fourths.
Usually children enjoy the leg portions while Mom
and Dad prefer the larger breast portions. Place the
chicken pieces and potatoes on each plate and top
with some of the pan drippings. Turn the squash
right-side up so they are like little bowls. Place the
squash on each plate and fill the squash with the
peas. Add a slice of butter to each.

Shopping List

Stock Items

___ Whole garlic   ___ Salt
___ Pepper   ___ Olive oil
___ Butter   ___ Shortening
___ Sugar   ___ Egg
___ Flour   ___ Baking powder
___ Milk   ___ Cinnamon

Special Purchases

___ 3-pound whole chicken
___ 2 table queen or acorn squash

___ 1 10-ounce package frozen peas
___ 1 basket fresh blueberries (1 pint)
___ 1 lemon

🍂 *Lemon Garlic Roast Chicken with Potatoes* 🍂

Preheat oven to 350 degrees.

3-pound whole chicken
1 lemon
8 cloves garlic (cloves are the small sections of
 the whole garlic)
Salt
Pepper
2 tablespoons olive oil
2 tablespoons butter
8 small red potatoes, peeled

Remove the inside pieces from the chicken and rinse it under cold water. Pat the chicken dry with paper towels. Cut the lemon into 8 wedge-shaped pieces. Rub the cut lemons over the outside of the chicken. Combine the lemon pieces with the garlic cloves and place inside the chicken. Generously sprinkle the outside of the chicken with salt and pepper. Place the chicken in a roasting pan and place the potatoes around it. In a small bowl, melt the butter in the microwave (about 1 minute) and add the olive oil to the butter. Pour the combined butter and oil over the chicken and the potatoes. Place the chicken in the preheated oven and cook for 1 hour and 15 minutes, basting frequently with the pan juices. Basting is easiest if you use a bulb baster. Simply insert the tip of the baster into the juices, squeeze the bulb and release it to draw the juices into the baster. Hold the tip over the chicken and squeeze the bulb again to release the juices over the chicken. The roasting pan may need to be tipped to allow the juices to collect in one corner before using the bulb baster.

🐾 Table Queen Squash with Green Peas 🐾

2 table queen or acorn squash
1 10-ounce package of frozen peas
Butter

Cut the squash in half. Using a spoon, scrape the inside of the squash to remove the seeds. Using a pan large enough to hold the four halves, place the squash open-side down in the pan. Add enough water to cover the bottom of the pan with about ¼ inch water. Place the squash in the oven and cook for 1 hour. Ten minutes before serving, prepare the peas according to the package instructions. When both the squash and peas are cooked, place the squash, cut-side up, on the plate, fill the bowl of the squash with peas and top the peas with a slice of butter.

🐾 Blueberry Buckle 🐾

½ cup shortening such as Crisco
½ cup sugar
1 egg

2 cups flour
2½ teaspoons baking powder
¼ teaspoon salt
½ cup milk
1 basket fresh blueberries (1 pint)

Topping

½ cup sugar
½ cup flour
½ teaspoon cinnamon
¼ cup butter

In a large bowl beat the egg with the electric beater. Add the shortening and sugar and beat well until they are blended and have a creamy texture.

Sift the flour, baking powder, and salt together onto a large piece of wax paper. Add half of the flour mixture to the creamed mixture and beat until well blended. Add the milk and beat again. Add the remaining flour mixture and beat again. Spread the batter evenly into an 11½ x 7½ x 1½ inch baking pan, well greased. Sprinkle the blueberries evenly over the batter.

In a small bowl, using a pastry blender, combine the remaining sugar, flour, cinnamon, and butter until they have a crumbly consistency and are well blended. Sprinkle the topping over the blueberries and bake in a preheated 350 degree oven for 45 to 50 minutes. Let it cool slightly before serving. To serve the Blueberry Buckle, cut it into squares and serve on plates. It may be topped with ice cream if desired.

Kids' Helps

Lemon Garlic Roast Chicken with Potatoes: Children can rub the outside of the chicken with the lemons and stuff the inside of the chicken with the combined lemon and garlic. They can sprinkle the chicken with salt and pepper and pour the butter and olive oil over the chicken and potatoes. Older children can peel the potatoes.

Table Queen Squash with Green Peas: These squash are a little bit difficult to work with but older children can scrape the seeds from the inside of the squash. Once the squash and peas are cooked, children can spoon the peas into the squash bowls.

Blueberry Buckle: If they know how, let the children crack the egg and empty it into the bowl. They can beat the egg and continue doing all the beating for this recipe. They can sift the dry ingredients. Let them sprinkle the blueberries over the batter and then sprinkle the topping over the blueberries.

Emergency Shopping List

Copy these pages and keep them in your wallet. Next time you're out too late and realize that you haven't given dinner a thought, simply pull this page out and head for the grocery store. Listed here are both the stock items and special purchases for the quickest and easiest menus found in *HomeMade Memories*. Review in your mind which of the items you think you already have at home and purchase what you will need to prepare the meal of your choice.

World's Quickest Dinner
Serves 4

Stock Items

___ White rice   ___ Salt
___ Pepper   ___ Dried rosemary
___ Flour   ___ Butter
___ Fresh parsley

Special Purchases

___ 2 boneless chicken breasts, 4 pieces
___ 2 medium carrots
___ 1 lemon
___ 1 orange
___ Vanilla ice cream
___ Hot fudge sauce

Sherried Chicken Dinner
Serves 4

Stock Items

___ Butter   ___ Salt
___ Pepper   ___ Flour

___ Fresh parsley   ___ Eggs
___ Vanilla

Special Purchases

___ 1 pound boneless chicken breasts
___ 1 pound asparagus
___ 1 lemon
___ Sherry
___ 1 12-ounce package chocolate chips
___ 2 large cartons whipping cream (1 pint each)

Octoberfest Dinner
Serves 6

Stock Items

___ Vanilla*   ___ Baking powder*
___ Cinnamon*   ___ Sugar*
___ Flour   ___ Butter
___ Eggs   ___ Salt
___ Pepper   ___ Prepared mustard

Special Purchases

___ 3 large green apples*
___ Whipping cream*
___ 3 medium potatoes
___ 1 onion
___ Sour cream
___ Sauerkraut
___ 6–8 Bockwurst or other German sausages

* If you are in a real hurry, skip the Apple-Topped German Cake
  and buy a frozen apple pastry.

Epilogue

My hope is that this book will stir your thinking about your childhood home and your present family. What takes place at home provides impor-tant balance as we face the world around us. You have the privilege of making that home environment as warm, loving, and nurturing as possible.

As you have read through *HomeMade Memories* and heard about the memories of my childhood and those of my friends, I am sure it has brought back many memories of your own. Some of those memo-ries may be good and others may be bad. Take some time to think about your own life and your mealtime memories right now.

What are some of the wonderful things you re-member about mealtimes in your childhood home? What can you do to keep those memories alive for your own family? What are some of the damaging or hurtful memories that may have been a part of your childhood mealtimes? What are you going to do now to keep from doing the same damaging things to your own family?

As you have read *HomeMade Memories* I hope that my ideas have sparked some creative thinking on your part. Before you forget, take a few moments to write down any new and creative ideas you have for making the mealtime special and how you are going to implement those ideas for your own family. In the future, continue being alert to other books, seminars, and magazine articles that feature additional ways to create homemade memories and add them to your list.

Now it is your turn to create homemade memories for your family. Cook some good meals, set a pretty table, and have encouraging conversation. Enjoy your home. Enjoy your food. Enjoy your family and friends!

Special Supplies for Making Homemade Memories

CLASS Book Service can provide many of the homemaking materials that are recommended in this book and others written by Marita Littauer. You may obtain a price list and other information by sending your request and a stamped, self-addressed business envelope to:

> CLASS Book Service
> 1645 S. Rancho Santa Fe, #102
> San Marcos, CA 92069

Charge orders may be placed by calling
1-800-433-6633

Other Good
Harvest House Reading

THE COMPLETE HOLIDAY ORGANIZER
by *Emilie Barnes*

The busy woman's answer to holiday planning, *The Complete Holiday Organizer* gives ideas and helpful hints to make celebration preparations easier. A brief history about each holiday will challenge you to begin your own family traditions and memories. A practical "how-to" book to help you get a handle on holiday organization.

THINGS HAPPEN WHEN WOMEN CARE
by *Emilie Barnes*

Things Happen When Women Care shows you how to carve out time for others by streamlining the details of daily living and home organization. This warm, insightful look at developing friendships and enlarging the boundaries of your personal ministry will give you the tools you need to start today on the great adventure of caring for others.

BEST FRIENDS FOR LIFE
by *V. Gilbert Beers*

One of life's most intimate human relationships is that of parent and child. Nothing is more important for a parent than knowing how to reach the heart of his or her child. Nothing is more important for a child than having parents who share their hearts. V. Gilbert Beers, father of five and bestselling author challenges parents to develop the kind of *talking relationship* with their children that will bring a lifelong friendship.